INFLATION

Also by P. J. Curwen

MANAGERIAL ECONOMICS
THE THEORY OF THE FIRM

With A. H. Fowler

ECONOMIC POLICY

INFLATION

P. J. Curwen

Senior Lecturer in Economics
Sheffield Polytechnic

M

First published 1976 by
THE MACMILLAN PRESS LTD
London and Basingstoke
Associated companies in New York Dublin
Melbourne Johannesburg and Madras

SBN 333 19240 0 (hard cover)
333 19241 9 (paper cover)

Printed in Great Britain by
THE ANCHOR PRESS LTD
Tiptree, Essex

Contents

PART 3
CAUSES OF THE CURRENT INFLATION

PART 4
CURES FOR THE CURRENT INFLATION

Introduction

This book is concerned primarily with analysing the causes of, and cures for, inflation. The nature of advanced industrial economies is, however, such as to require considerable attention to be paid simultaneously to the other principal objectives of economic policy, namely the level of employment, the state of the balance of payments, and the rate of economic growth. One particular concern of this book must therefore be to explore the relationship between the rate of inflation and these three other objectives, with the greatest emphasis being placed upon the relationship between inflation and employment.

For a period of approximately two decades between the First and Second World Wars the overriding fact of economic life was an historically high level of unemployment, which proved largely impervious to the impact of control techniques which had their origins in the very different conditions of the late nineteenth century. Then in 1936 Keynes published *The General Theory* and seemingly demonstrated for all time that involuntary unemployment is an unnecessary evil which lies within the powers of any enlightened government to eradicate in its entirety.

At the time it seemed to most of those who read *The General Theory* that it contained precepts for the management of the economy which would ensure continued prosperity. The effects of sustained high levels of employment upon the price level were paid scant attention since the prevailing trend of prices during the 1930s was downwards rather than the reverse, and there was little reason to foresee that the eradication of long-term unemployment would coincide with continued inflation. Certainly it was well known that the U.K. economy had previously undergone several protracted periods of inflation, but these had all been characterised by an increase in the money supply far in excess of the rate of productivity growth. Fiscal policy, on the other hand, was expected to function without a strong inflationary bias, and it must surely have seemed inconceivable to policy-makers during the 1930s that the economy would ever develop the alarming characteristic known popularly as 'stagflation' – the conjunction of a stagnant economy and acclerating inflation.

During the course of the Second World War the economy attained a state of full employment, and this was sustained during the early post-war years, somewhat to the surprise of the authorities who were anticipating the recurrence of industrial depression. This historically high level of employment was, however, accompanied by relatively mild inflation which resulted in periodic crises in the balance of payments. The stock response of the authorities in these circumstances was, first, to cut back on aggregate demand in order to ameliorate the payments imbalance, and subsequently to expand aggregate demand in order to mitigate the resultant increase in unemployment, a procedure which became known as the 'stop–go' cycle.

During the 1950s the first serious work began to appear on the problems generated by on-going inflation, with particular reference to the relationship between inflation and unemployment. As we shall go on to discover in detail in the main body of the text, the most lasting impact was made by the discovery of the 'Phillips Curve' which purported to show a stable inverse relationship between the rate of change of prices and the level of unemployment. This relationship was seized upon for policy purposes since it apparently put the authorities in the happy position of being able to predict how much inflation would be associated with any given level of employment. Furthermore, it indicated that inflation could be controlled by recourse to periodic sharp doses of unemployment.

But in 1966 the rate of inflation began to speed up appreciably, and when eventually the then Conservative Government decided that a heavy dose of unemployment could no longer be postponed, its imposition had no visible impact upon the inflation rate whatsoever.

Indeed inflation began to accelerate upwards even more swiftly, apparently quite independently of the level of employment.

That both inflation and employment could get worse simultaneously was indeed a new departure in the history of economics. Academics and economic advisers hurried back to their respective ivory towers and corridors of power to contemplate what had gone wrong and what could be done about it. Alternative, and often conflicting, versions of the inflationary process poured forth from all sides. Meanwhile things got steadily worse with price inflation reaching 20 per cent at the end of 1974. The imminent collapse of the U.K. economy was prophesied by economists and politicians of all leanings, some with infinite regret and some with little short of outright glee, but the economy struggled on into 1975. At the time of writing, early in 1975, the economy shows signs of acute schizophrenia. On the one hand, there are widespread bankruptcies, negligible industrial investment, the largest budget deficit in history and wage claims averaging well over 20 per cent while, on the other hand, the Stock Market is rising sharply, Building Societies are recording unparalleled inflows of savings, and exports are booming.

Now, more than ever, it is essential to clarify what inflation means, how it affects the distribution of income, what causes it, and how it can be cured. Unfortunately, as will become clear in the course of this book, the state of economic science is still far too primitive to give a cast-iron answer to the vital question of what causes inflation. Nor is there any concensus amongst those who claim to have some expertise in the area about the policies which the current crisis demands. Under the circumstances it is hardly surprising that the general public is extremely confused about the whole issue.

This book lays no claim to making an original contribution to the analysis of inflation. Instead it serves what the author believes to be a fundamentally important purpose, namely to chart a path through the morass of literature on inflation (by no means all of which is encompassed by this volume despite its sizeable bibliography) in order to render the main issues comprehensible to those who lack the necessary technical training in economics to read source material at first hand. Curiously, perhaps, no other attempt to do this has as yet been published so far as the author is aware. Certainly many articles have appeared in the newspapers and in, for example, bank journals, but these invariably have an axe to grind and, for reasons of brevity, tend to treat as established fact many assertions of dubious validity. The author himself has no wish to lay claim to complete impartiality, but seeks to explore every point of view which currently has a widespread following, in the hope that the reader will at least be able to decide for himself on the basis of all known facts.

The bulk of the text consists of two main sections, the first of which considers the causes of inflation and the second of which considers the cures. The opening section of the book is, however, the most fundamental to the issue at hand. This contains the basic statistical data used in the book, an explanation of what precisely the term inflation means and how it is measured, and an analysis of why inflation needs to be controlled.

After completing this book the reader may well feel a sense of disappointment that there are no easy answers to the control of inflation, and that he cannot put the Chancellor of the Exchequer's constant policy switches down to sheer political cussedness. On the other hand, he may well feel pleased that the book confirms his prejudices about, for example, the inefficacy of prices-and-incomes policies. No matter, however, which school of thought the reader supports he will at the very least have the satisfaction of being armed with extensive ammunition with which to confound his opponents in debate, and that at least is some small reward for his labours in working his way through the pages which follow.

This book is intended primarily for all those who have completed a basic course in economics. Although parts of the book can be read without difficulty by the first-year student or, indeed, by the layman, the nature of the literature surveyed makes it necessary to raise many issues, especially in the theoretical sections, of a technically complex kind. It is hoped that final-year undergraduates and post-graduates will find this book of value as a basis for their detailed reading of source material. The book is fully referenced in order to assist both advanced students and lecturers with the otherwise time-consuming task of tracking down a widely diffused literature.

By way of conclusion I wish to thank my colleagues Nick Foster and David Holmes for their careful reviews of earlier drafts of this book, and also David Pearce of Leicester University and John Burton of Kingston Polytechnic for acting as referees. All remaining errors are, however, entirely my own responsibility.

P.J.C.

Part 1
The Basic Issues

1 Inflation: Its Meaning and Measurement

Definitions

An economy is commonly regarded as suffering from inflation if it is undergoing a period of continuously rising prices. The upward adjustment of prices is, however, subject to delays of varying duration. Prices, for example, may be held down deliberately in the short run by the authorities, or alternatively, if demand is too great to be satisfied by current domestic production at current prices, it is possible for the necessary balancing of demand and supply to result not through rising domestic prices but through either the running down of stocks or through the purchase of additional imported goods. Furthermore, it is possible for the prices of individual products to be held constant, even at a time of sharply rising costs, by recourse to a policy of deterioration in size or quality.

For these various reasons it is necessary to measure inflation over periods sufficiently long as to eliminate any bias arising from purely short-term phenomena. Most commonly, the period of choice is one calendar year, and the rate of inflation is then stated as the percentage increase in prices on any given date as compared to the same date one year previously. In addition, it is now the custom to publish figures showing the percentage change in prices on a monthly basis. Such figures can often give a totally distorted view of the state of the economy. Perhaps that is why they are so frequently cited by politicians! However, since the prices of all goods and services do not rise simultaneously and by an equal amount[1] it is also necessary to assess the extent to which the general price level has risen by utilising some form of price index, designed to measure changes in the pattern of household consumption expenditure.

In the United Kingdom there is a *General*[2] *Index of Retail Prices* and a *Consumer Price Index*. Both indices incorporate a (different) cross-section of those goods and services which are most frequently purchased by an 'average' household. Clearly, however, it is unsatisfactory simply to note the extent to which the prices of pre-selected goods and services change over time, because we would normally expect households to alter their consumption patterns as some goods rise in price relative to others. Hence the importance of expenditure upon individual items constituting the index relative to total expenditure must be adjusted in line with changes in purchasing behaviour. This is done by multiplying each item in the index by a 'weight' which reflects the importance of expenditure on that item in relation to the average household's budget, and thereby arriving at a 'weighted index'. The weights are altered in response to changes in purchasing behaviour which can be discerned through analysis of the results of surveys of household expenditure. Major changes in the definition of individual items in the Retail Price Index are recommended by the Retail Prices Index Advisory Committee.[3]

The most obvious drawback to the above process is that there is no such entity as an 'average' household in real life, and no system of weights can ever hope to reflect the purchasing behaviour of unusually wealthy or unusually poor households.[4] Furthermore, any household, irrespective of its income, can attempt to protect itself against the effects of inflation, suffered by other households living on equivalent incomes, by shopping around for bargains or by increasing the value of fixed-price contracts into which it enters. Except at times when interest rates are fluctuating wildly, an increased mortgage will, for example, perform this desirable function. In any event the capital-repayment element of a mortgage remains fixed in money terms over time even if the interest-repayment element is fluctuating.

Some Statistical Data

It is appropriate at this point to consider the statistical data on price changes. However, rather than treat these figures in isolation, it is desirable to present the corresponding data on the other major variables which will constantly recur within the main body of the text. Thus Tables 1.1 and 1.2 below also contain data on wages, earnings, profits, employment, vacancies and stoppages of work. Data on these variables is available from two main sources, the first of which is the *Department of Employment Gazette* which contains official government figures, and the second of which is the *National Institute Economic Review* published by the National Institute of Economic and Social Research. Differences in the base years chosen for the price indices make direct comparisons impossible, although the over-all picture remains unchanged.

TABLE 1.1

(1970=100)	*Weekly wage rates* (*All industries*)	*Weekly earnings** (*All industries*)	*Retail prices*	*Profits of companies and public corporations**
1962	66·2	58·5	72·4	65·0
1963	68·6	60·8	73·8	74·0
1964	71·5	65·1	76·7	81·9
1965	74·6	70·0	80·2	85·8
1966	78·0	74·5	83·2	84·7
1967	81·0	77·0	85·2	86·8
1968	86·4	83·2	89·3	99·5
1969	91·0	89·7	93·9	98·8
1970	100·0	100·0	100·0	100·0
1971	112·9	111·2	109·5	109·3
1972	127·9	125·1	117·0	125·0
1973	145·4	142·4	126·8	156·4
1974	173·1	167·5	147·0	177·7
1973 I	137·6	134·7	122·2	153·4
1973 II	142·5	139·9	125·2	152·0
1973 III	149·0	145·0	127·7	157·9
1973 IV	152·5	149·9	131·8	162·3
1974 I	156·7	149·0	137·2	178·9
1974 II	164·8	159·4	145·3	178·8
1974 III	179·6	173·8	149·4	181·4
1974 IV	191·3	187·8	156·7	171·7
1975 I	203·8	196·4	165·6	188·3

* Seasonally adjusted.

SOURCE: *National Institute Economic Review.*

TABLE 1.2

	Retail prices (1962 = 100)*	Unemployed		Adult unfilled vacancies		Number of stoppages	Workers involved (000s)	Working days lost (000s)
		Percentage rate	Number (000s)	Percentage rate	Number (000s)			
1964	107·0	1·56	372·2	0·96	220·8	2524	883	2277
1965	112·1	1·32	317·0	1·15	265·1	2354	876	2925
1966	116·5	1·37	330·9	1·10	254·8	1937	544	2398
1967	119·4	2·19	521·0	0·76	174·0	2116	734	2787
1968	125·0	2·33	549·4	0·82	188·0	2378	2258	4690
1969	131·8	2·30	543·8	0·87	199·6	3116	1665	6846
1970	140·2	2·48	582·2	0·81	185·8	3906	1801	10980
1971	153·4	3·25	758·4	0·56	129·0	2228	1178	13551
1972	164·3	3·59	844·1	0·64	145·3	2497	1734	23909
1973	179·4	2·58	597·9	1·31	303·9	2873	1528	7197
1974	208·2	2·60	599·7	1·30	298·8	2882	1605	14740
	(Jan 1974 = 100)†							
1974 Jan	100·0	2·70	605·6	1·24	285·4			
Mar	102·6	2·56	590·2	1·16	266·5			
June	108·7	2·20	515·8	1·46	336·4			
Sep	111·0	2·80	647·1	1·32	307·2			
Dec	116·9	Not recorded		Not recorded				
1975 Mar	124·3	3·30	768·4	0·78	178·0			
June	137·1	3·58	831·8	0·70	159·0			
Sep								
Dec								

* Monthly averages.

† This new base will be used exclusively from January 1975.

SOURCE: *Department of Employment Gazette*.

The Money Illusion

Before we can apply the above statistics to the analysis of inflation certain additional factors need to be given further consideration. In the first place we need to distinguish clearly between the 'money' and 'real' effects of changes in wages and prices. The index of weekly wage rates in Table 1.1 measures changes in 'money income', often referred to as 'nominal income', that is income measured in currency units. 'Real income', on the other hand, is a measure of the quantity of goods and services which the individual can buy with his available money income, and therefore expressly allows for changes in the price level. Any upward movement in the general price level necessarily diminishes the real value of a fixed stock of money, the reverse holding true for a downward movement. Clearly, therefore, a household can only be said to be 'better off' in real terms if its money income is increasing more rapidly than the over-all level of prices of the things which it buys. However, we must also make express allowance for the fact that the average household's income is greatly diminished at source by way of deductions for income tax, National Insurance, and so forth. Hence it is more meaningful to talk of a household becoming better off (enjoying a rising *standard of living*) where its *disposable* income is rising at a faster rate than the price level. Of course, most households receive back from the authorities a flow of free goods and services in return for any income deducted at source. Hence their standard of living is also affected by the real value of surrendered income, that is by changes in the access to freely provided goods and services which they obtain in return for any given amount of income deducted at source.

It is clear from the above discussion that at times of inflation an increase in gross money income considerably overstates the rise in a household's standard of living. Failure to take account of this is known as *money illusion*. It is commonly argued in the context of the current inflation that, whereas the average household failed to differentiate between money income and real income, and hence suffered from money illusion during the 1950s and 1960s, it ceased so to do during the 1970s. The implications of the disappearance of money illusion for the analysis of inflation will be a recurrent topic in subsequent sections of this book.

Price Inflation versus Wage Inflation

So far we have talked about inflation exclusively in terms of upwards movements in the Retail Price Index. At the present time, however, it is becoming increasingly common to measure inflation by reference to the index either of wage rates or of earnings, both of which are set out in Table 1.1. There are two reasons for this preference which are of particular interest. First, it should be noted that all those who subscribe to the view that trade unions are the major cause of inflation seek to support their arguments by reference to the pace of wage inflation. Secondly, since it is in the nature of things, for reasons explained below, that wage inflation is always more rapid than price inflation, it is possible for 'opposition' politicians and journalists to make more political capital from the wage-rate index than from the price index. Of late it has also been true that the current very high rate of wage inflation has enabled those commentators so inclined to haunt us with the spectre of impending hyperinflation.

During the 1960s the rate of wage inflation did not differ by more than a few per cent from that of price inflation. However, this is no longer the case. In December 1974, measured on an annual basis, the rate of price inflation was 19·1 per cent whereas that of wage inflation was 29·1 per cent. It is, therefore, of some interest to enquire at this point how it is that wage inflation can outstrip price inflation by such a wide margin, and to ask further whether this can be interpreted at face value to mean that real wages are really rising on average by 10 per cent per annum. The following factors are relevant in this context.

(*a*) If we examine the indices of wage rates and of profits in Table 1.1 it appears superficially that profits have risen at a faster rate even than wages. Both magnitudes are, however, measured in nominal rather than in real terms, and both are measured before tax is deducted. In subsequent sections of this book we hope to demonstrate that real profits were virtually non-existent in 1974 whereas real wages rose in part at the expense of profits. In other words, rapidly rising nominal wages were not fully adjusted for through rising prices, with the result that profit margins were squeezed.

(*b*) Wage settlements towards the latter end of 1974 were unusually large because they covered groups such as local-authority manual workers which included a high proportion of lower-paid employees whose rates were being brought up to the target of £30 per week proposed as a minimum wage by the Trades Union Congress. In addition certain settlements included an element of back-pay which appeared on P.A.Y.E. slips as a lump-sum addition to basic rates. Neither of these factors was reflected in commensurate price rises at the time, although clearly such rises are simply being delayed by the need, for example, for the nationalised industries to seek ratification of proposed price rises.

(*c*) In addition, there was a threshold provision built into a large number of wage agreements covering the period October 1973 to October 1974 whereby any price rise above the threshold level subsequently led to a wage rise of equal proportions during the following month. Hence, in these cases, workers so covered maintained the percentage differential between the initially negotiated wage increase and the 7 per cent threshold price level, even when prices rose above that level. By the end of 1974 wage rates were, on average, some 13 per cent above the levels originally negotiated as a direct consequence of the threshold provision.

(*d*) Increases in productivity also need to be taken into account. In this context it is appropriate to enquire whether wages can increase without causing any resultant reduction in profits, even if prices also remain unchanged. This can be illustrated as follows: an improvement in productivity means that a larger quantity of output can be obtained from a fixed stock of labour and machinery. If this increased level of output were to be sold at unchanged prices then revenues would rise. Now, for profits also to remain unchanged in these circumstances, costs must increase by the same amount as revenues. But if the stock of both capital and labour is fixed then such a rise in costs can only be the consequence of increases in the hourly wage rates paid to labour inputs, once due allowance has been made for the additional cost of raw materials needed in order to expand production and for the increased running cost of machinery.

In other words wages can rise at times of increasing productivity without consequently forcing firms to raise their prices in order to protect their profit levels. Of course, any benefits arising from increased productivity can, in principle, be shared out between wages and profits. It would appear, however, that in 1974 the entire increase in productivity was absorbed through increased wages. This was, of course, in addition to the redistribution out of profits into wages mentioned in (*a*) above.

In the light of the above factors it is hardly surprising that money wages outstripped prices during 1974. The relationship between these two variables is not, however, by any means constant, and it is probable that the differential will have narrowed during 1975. What is fundamentally at issue, however, for the purposes of analysing inflation, is the impact which this differential has upon the average worker's standard of living. Now we all know perfectly well that *real* wages did not go up on average by 10 per cent during 1974, and the reason is because the relationship between gross and disposable income is prone to fluctuations which stem principally from the effects of the income-tax threshold. Below a certain minimum level of gross earnings a household pays no income tax whatsoever, and above a certain threshold level it pays tax at more than the standard rate. But since the various tax thresholds tend to remain fairly static over time, rapid inflation has the effect of lifting increasing numbers of households both into the tax-paying category and also into the higher tax brackets. (National Insurance contributions *also* increase as they are earnings-related.) As a result the proportion of gross income left post-tax diminishes over time except in those years when tax thresholds are adjusted. Given that the minimum rate of income tax is currently 35 per cent it is obvious that, *on average*, disposable incomes do not in practice rise much faster than prices, if at all, even when there exists a significant differential between gross wage rates and prices.

2 The Impact of Inflation

Introduction

If one studies the history of economic policy over the post-war years it rapidly becomes apparent that, with the possible exception of the Conservative Government's 'lame-duck' policy in 1971, the control of inflation has never been given top priority as an objective. The primary goal of all governments during this period, including the current Labour administration which ought by now to have learned its lesson, has been the pursuit of full employment at almost any cost. It almost goes without saying that these costs have indeed been considerable. During the 1950s and 1960s the main impact of full-employment policies was borne by the balance of payments as excessive imports were sucked in by the continued high level of domestic aggregate demand. The resultant 'stop–go' sequence of policy measures with its attendant uncertainties served to restrain the rate of growth of the economy. Additionally, the high level of aggregate demand resulted in continued mild inflation, but the governments of the day did not consider this too high a price to pay for the electoral benefits of negligible unemployment.

During the 1950s and 1960s, although it was recognised that inflation served to redistribute income among differing groups within the economy, the impact during any single year was too slight to warrant concerted action by the aggrieved parties, besides which money illusion was so widespread that few people made any explicit allowance for the erosive impact of continued inflation upon real returns. On the other hand, there grew up a widespread belief in the beneficial effects of mild inflation. In particular, it was argued that inflation was beneficial for employment and for growth. In these respects the nub of the argument was that inflation would serve to redistribute wealth to that sector most likely to use it productively. The legacy of *The General Theory* had been to inculcate a belief in deficit financing to stimulate aggregate demand. This in turn caused businessmen to expect demand to be buoyant in the future with its attendant promise of rising prices and hence rising profits. Their natural response would be to invest in new capacity, to expand the work-force, and to commit large sums to research and development, invention and innovation – hence the alleged beneficial impact upon growth and employment.

The evidence seems to lend limited support to the contention that mild inflation promotes economic growth.[1] Nevertheless there is no evidence to suggest anything other than that inflation running in double figures creates an adverse environment for growth and employment. In view of this it is fair to argue that the current inflation has few beneficial effects. On the other hand, it is alleged that its adverse effects are many and varied, as indicated in the paragraphs below.

Redistributional Effects

The adverse impact of inflation is most commonly associated with those living on fixed money incomes, since the real value of their incomes must constantly decline. Groups such as pensioners are generally the members of society least able to bear such an erosion of their purchasing power, and the evidence clearly demonstrates that they suffer badly during prolonged mild inflation. Curiously, perhaps, pensioners have not suffered in the longer term. This is because the onset of rapid inflation has led to such strong pressure being put upon governments that especial care is now being taken to protect pensioners' standards of living. The same does not, however, apply to those who have retired on fixed incomes which are funded by the private rather than the public sector. Many occupational pension schemes, for example, have no built-in provisions for cost-of-living increases, and many retired couples rely upon the yield of fixed-interest investments to keep them going. Organisations as well as individuals are affected in this way. Charities, for example, tend to find that their incomes rise only slowly in money terms while at the same time the causes which they espouse grow increasingly expensive to fund.

Rapid inflation may also serve to redistribute income from the poorly organised to the well organised. In the annual wage-bargaining round the former rarely obtain the same level of pay rises which large, rich, unions can extract from employers – if necessary by threat of strike action. Furthermore, even if the poorly organised, and hence often the poorly paid, do manage to obtain percentage wage increases as large as those granted to their better-organised counterparts, the absolute value of such increases will be correspondingly less.

One curious aspect of the current inflation is, however, that it has tended to redistribute income from private-sector to public-sector employees. During the 1960s, when inflation was relatively mild, public-sector employees found themselves bargaining with governments determined to hold down wages as it were 'by example' (which the private sector largely ignored) rather than with an employers' association willing, if at all possible, to pass on wage rises through increased prices. The financial difficulties of the private sector in 1973–4 meant, however, that private-sector wage demands had to be reduced whereas public-sector employees, taking advantage of successive weak governments, went on strike and obtained wage awards of unparalleled munificence.

At times of rapid inflation it may pay to go heavily into debt. When a loan of given size is repaid, its real value will have fallen below that prevailing at the time the loan was made, and this percentage loss of real value must be deducted from the interest rate being charged in order to determine the true cost of the loan. Any rate of inflation therefore diminishes the return on a loan, but when the inflation rate rises to the point at which it exceeds the rates commonly being charged on loans (which is currently the case), virtually all loans can end up earning a (sometimes considerable) negative real rate of return. In other words, at the present time anyone who saves with a bank or Building Society is effectively subsidising someone else's expenditure. The debtor–creditor relationship does, however, involve us in certain value judgements. In particular we may note that the largest debtor of all is the government which finds the real servicing cost of financing the National Debt ever less burdensome. Inflation also eases the burden of mortgage repayments, which some may argue is a desirable trend.

Inflation may impinge upon the corporate sector in a variety of ways. One possibility is that there may be a redistribution out of gross profits and into incomes (particularly at times when some kind of price control is in operation). This results from the fact that there must come a time in every market, especially where international competition is significant, when purchasers will decide to withdraw their custom in the face of continuing price rises (witness the new car market in late 1974). Meanwhile, the unions may continue to exert upwards pressure upon wage rates, in the face of which the employers may prefer to capitulate rather than be subjected to a costly strike.

A further problem has to do with stock appreciation. Companies, for the most part, use the first-in–first-out inventory method whereby, at the time when they are used in production, stocks are costed at buying-in (historic) prices even though the replacement cost of the same item may be significantly higher. This has the effect of artificially raising nominal profit levels because the price at which the product sells will itself have inflated well above the level prevailing when the stock was bought in. This accounts in large part for the very rapid rise in the profits index in Table 1.1 above. But these nominal profits are then subjected to corporate taxation with the result that the residual, post-tax profit may be insufficient to cover the cost of replacing at *current* prices the stock used up during the previous accounting period. In other words, a large nominal profit on an historic-cost basis may turn out to be a negative real profit on a replacement-cost basis. There can be little doubt that this is exactly what transpired for many companies during 1974, with the result that the Chancellor of the Exchequer was obliged to introduce measures in his November Budget to ease the burden upon the corporate sector.

A falling, or negative, real rate of profit itself produces further effects. Some firms may face a liquidity crisis and go out of business. Others may cut back severely their investment programmes because of uncertainty about the future. Alternatively, firms with spare cash resources may prefer to invest them, not in manufacturing concerns, but in speculative activity of various kinds. Once again it is clear that the speculative boom in property values in 1972–3 was partly funded in this way.

So far we have made a number of assertions about the likely effects of inflation upon the distribution of income. It is therefore appropriate at this point to consider the empirical evidence relating to this matter. Such evidence is, unfortunately, rather sparse with respect to the United Kingdom. Of the early studies Lydall,[2] covering the period 1949–51, Brittain,[3] covering the period 1951–6, and Lynes,[4] covering the period 1948–61, all found some evidence of inflation impinging more heavily upon the poorer sections of society than upon the rich, whereas Seers,[5] and Allen,[6] found the opposite to hold true. More recently Tipping,[7] covering the period 1956–66, found that the poorest households suffered more from inflation than middle-income and high-income households. The most up-to-date study is that by Muellbauer,[8] covering the period 1964–72. He concludes that 'for more than twenty years relative consumer price changes have had an inegalitarian basis' and that 'the degree of bias has recently been increasing'. This he suggests is due in particular to (1) the impact of rising food prices which by their very nature are highly regressive in income terms since every household, irrespective of income, has to eat, and (2) to the capital gains sustained by house-owners but not by tenants.

If we turn to consider the evidence from the United States we find that there is some support for the viewpoint that inflation has had only a very mild impact upon the distribution of income.[9] Elsewhere Budd[10] suggests, on the basis of evidence collected over the entire post-war period, that there has been 'a gain by the middle and upper part of the distribution, relative to the lower groups and the upper tail', although once again not of any great significance. The comment about the upper tail of the distribution is, however, of particular interest because it contradicts the oft-voiced view that the wealthier you are the less you are affected by inflation. As Bach and Stephenson point out 'simple conclusions that inflation is good for the rich and bad for the poor, or other comparable statements, need to be viewed with considerable doubt'.[11] Their study confirms our previously stated hypothesis that continued inflation redistributes income from profit-earners to wage-earners,[12] a shift which they argue has been 'substantial' over the past few years. They also suggest that there has been a sizeable redistribution of income from creditors to debtors.

In this latter respect Bach and Stephenson argue that the major redistribution has been from households (holders of the National

Debt) to the government (issuers of the National Debt). They also identify a significant redistribution within the household sector.

> Both the very poor and the very rich are more exposed to inflation than the middle income groups. The very poor have few debts (no one will lend to them) and hold what few assets they have partly in monetary forms. The rich also have relatively few debts (though for quite different reasons) and hold a substantial part of their wealth in bonds. . . . Middle income families tend to be heavily in debt (mainly to buy houses, autos and the like) and have the bulk of their assets in such forms. . . . The other main conclusion is that old people are heavily exposed to inflation on asset-debt account; they have few debts and hold a relatively high proportion of their assets in fixed-value forms. Conversely young families are generally heavily in debt.[13]

Further confirmation of the redistribution of income from profit-earners to wage-earners, but this time with respect to the United Kingdom, is presented by Glyn and Sutcliffe[14] in the form of Table 2.1.

TABLE 2.1 *Share of profits in company net output*, 1950–70 (per cent)*

1950–4		1955–9		1960–4		1965–9
25·2		22·8		21·0		17·4
1964	1965	1966	1967	1968	1969	1970
21·2	20·2	17·6	18·1	16·8	14·2	12·1

*Company profits as a proportion of profits and wages paid.

According to Glyn and Sutcliffe's figures the share of profits was almost halved between 1964 and 1970. This, they argue, was due to the 'squeezing of profit margins between money wage increases on the one hand and progressively more severe international competition on the other'.[15] They interpret these results to imply that 'British capitalism has suffered such a dramatic decline in profitability that it is now literally fighting for survival'. Other commentators take a more sanguine view of the problem although there is considerable support for Glyn and Sutcliffe's basic proposition. Paníc and Close[16] argue, for example, that 'there has been a decline in the rate of profit in the manufacturing sector over the last two decades. The fall has probably been the inevitable result of the growth of productive capacity and, consequently, growing competition, both domestic and international'. However, 'most of the observed deterioration took place in the 1950s. Since then there has been some decline, but it could in no sense be described as dramatic.'[17] Burgess and Webb similarly conclude that 'All the series indicate that the rate of return on capital has experienced a secular decline, at least throughout the 1960s, whether profitability is measured before or after tax. Although different conceptual approaches may slightly modify the results obtained, the marked downward trend is apparent regardless of the method adopted or the company grouping considered.'[18]

However, these findings must be treated with considerable caution because profitability is greatly dependent upon the changing tax burden on companies. The relative impact of changing taxation provisions upon wages and profits is explored in some detail by Wilkinson and Turner.[19] Their findings are presented in Table 2.2.[20] The figures in Table 2.2 suggest strongly that the taxation system operated during the 1950s and 1960s in favour of profits at the expense of incomes. This can be seen more clearly by examining total corporate profits as a percentage of aggregate wages and salaries as is shown in Table 2.3.[21]

TABLE 2.2 *The incidence of direct taxation on corporate income and employment incomes*

Percentage of income taken as taxation from:	Corporate profits		Wages and salaries
	Excluding tax on dividends	Including tax on dividends	
1949–52	36·5	45·6	9·8
1953–6	31·5	40·1	8·9
1957–60	25·9	35·2	10·6
1961–4	22·0	33·1	12·3
1965–8	19·0	30·9	15·5

TABLE 2.3 *Total corporate profits as a percentage of aggregate wages and salaries*

	Before tax	After tax*
1949–52	41·6	25·0
1953–6	39·7	26·1
1957–60	39·5	28·7
1961–4	37·6	28·6
1965–8	37·2	30·2

* Including tax on dividends.

A recent study confirms the above findings and also brings them up to date. In this study King uses a complex tax model which yields the results that are shown in Table 2.4.[22] King notes first, that if cyclical movements are taken into account then 'while there has been a long-run decline in the share of pre-tax conventional gross profits, this has coincided with changes in taxes and investment incentives which have left the share of conventional gross profits after tax virtually unchanged'.[23] These divergent trends reflect the decline in the tax rate levied upon companies as set out in Table 2.2 above. Of particular interest is the trend since the late 1960s. Between 1969 and 1971 all profit-share measures except that taken pre-tax showed sharp downwards movements, but the sharpest fall was in the measure which incorporates stock appreciation,

TABLE 2.4 *Profit shares in U.K. manufacturing* 1950–73 (per cent)*

	Conventional gross profits		Post-tax net of depreciation‡	Post-tax, net of depreciation and stock appreciation
	Pre-tax	Post-tax†		
1956	33·0	25·3	20·0	17·8
1957	32·7	25·2	19·7	18·0
1958	31·8	25·4	19·8	20·0
1959	33·1	27·0	21·7	20·9
1960	32·6	26·7	21·5	20·6
1961	30·5	25·1	19·6	18·7
1962	29·4	24·5	18·9	19·0
1963	31·3	26·6	21·1	19·8
1964	32·2	27·2	21·9	20·8
1965	31·3	27·8	22·5	20·8
1966	29·8	26·0	20·4	18·7
1967	29·6	25·8	19·9	19·2
1968	30·6	26·6	20·7	18·0
1969	28·1	24·5	18·4	15·3
1970	26·3	23·7	17·4	12·4
1971	26·5	24·4	16·4	12·1
1972	26·9	23·6	17·1	12·5
1973	29·4	26·4	20·6	12·5

* Excluding metal manufacture. Profit shares are calculated as the ratio of profits (however defined) to profits plus income from employment which comprises wages and salaries plus employers' national insurance and pension-fund contributions.

† Post-tax profits are equal to dividends and interest payments before deduction of income tax, plus gross retained profits and investment grants.

‡ At replacement cost.

although it had previously proved remarkably stable. These years were characterised by unusually high stock appreciation which was counted in its entirety as taxable income. Hence tax bills were particularly severe at this time, and the recovery in gross profits between 1971–3 was for similar reasons much reduced when continued high stock appreciation was taken into account.

The current significance of stock appreciation as a component of gross pre-tax profitability is shown by King in his estimates of the proportion of total tax liability due to taxation of stock appreciation (see Table 2.5).[24] The National Institute of Economic and Social Research has made some tentative estimates for the first half of 1974 on the basis of the definitions used in King's study.[25] According to their figures 1974 was similar to 1973 in all respects bar one.

TABLE 2.5 *Proportion of total tax liability due to taxation of stock appreciation (per cent)*

1956	1957	1958	1959	1960	1961	1962	1963	1964
10·1	8·0	−1·1	5·0	5·8	7·3	−1·6	12·2	10·2
1965	**1966**	**1967**	**1968**	**1969**	**1970**	**1971**	**1972**	**1973**
15·1	13·9	7·2	24·0	29·2	60·5	37·5	47·9	120·6

In the first quarter of 1974 post-tax profits net of depreciation and stock appreciation apparently fell to −0·3 per cent, and rose in the second quarter to a mere 2·1 per cent. In view of this there can be little doubt that 1974 witnessed a redistribution out of profits and into wages and salaries. What is not clear, however, is the likely trend of profits over the second half of the current decade. During 1974 a considerable debate waged as to whether or not stock appreciation should legitimately be regarded as taxable profit. It would appear from the steps taken by the Chancellor of the Exchequer as part of his November 1974 Budget that profit arising out of stock appreciation is to be regarded as something of a special case where taxation is concerned, but the longer-term redistributional implications of the Chancellor's stop-gap measures are as yet unclear.

Over all, then, there is considerable evidence available to support the contention that inflation, especially when it is rapid, serves to redistribute income between different sections of the community. This statement does not, of course, make explicit any value judgement as to whether or not such a redistribution is socially desirable. Indeed the fundamental issue in this respect is not so much the question as to the social desirability of any redistribution, but that this redistribution occurs in a manner which is not *actively* influenced by the authorities in the cause either of social justice or of economic growth.

However, rapid inflation is not to be indicted solely on account of its redistributive effects, important though they may well be. The onset of rapid inflation inevitably summons to mind the spectre of hyperinflation which leads, in the majority of cases, to the breakdown of economic, social and political life. Hyperinflation, which is characterised above all else by the replacement of money units by, for example, cigarette units as a store of value and unit of account, is not a new phenomenon either to Europe or to the developing countries. With U.K. nominal earnings rising at nearly 30 per cent on an annual basis at the end of 1974 it is hardly surprising that talk of hyperinflation has become rife. However, the experience of previous hyperinflations seems to suggest that it invariably has its origins in the uncontrolled printing of money, a cardinal sin so far avoided by successive U.K. governments. It is therefore extremely debatable that we are anywhere near the brink of the hyperinflation abyss, although it is foolish to underestimate the tremendous adjustment required of an economy experiencing a 'mere' twenty to thirty per cent price inflation.

International Effects

One other important matter has to do, not with the domestic impact of rapid inflation within the United Kingdom, but with its impact upon the balance of payments. In the international arena it is *relative* prices which matter and not absolute prices. The total value of both imports and exports is determined by the prices at which goods and services are traded, the quantities shipped, and the exchange rate between the currencies of the countries in question. Let us suppose for illustrative purposes that the total import bill and the total export bill are initially equal one to the other (in equilibrium). If U.K. prices then rise on domestic sales this will cause the prices of U.K. exports to rise correspondingly. Assuming no movement in the exchange rate[26] and no change in the prices of equivalent goods produced abroad, the volume and, as is generally the case, the value[27] of U.K. exports will decline because they will have become relatively more expensive as compared to substitute goods produced abroad, and this will have the effect of sucking in more imports. This in turn will necessarily raise the import bill because the price of imports expressed in sterling will remain unaffected by the increase in volume. Hence the over-all effect of a faster rate of inflation for the United Kingdom than for her trading partners will almost certainly be a deficit on the current account of the U.K. balance of payments. Of course, should U.K. prices rise more slowly than prices abroad, then the deficit becomes converted to a probable surplus.

For all of these various reasons outlined above rapid inflation gives cause for concern. Why then, one is obviously tempted to ask, have the authorities invariably fought shy of introducing stringent anti-inflationary policies? The answer, of course, is to be found in our previous discussion of the relative priority of economic objectives. If, for example, the eradication of unemployment is assigned a higher priority than the eradication of inflation, and further, if less inflation means more unemployment (and vice versa) an economy is likely to end up with everyone at work combined with spiralling prices. In the chapters which follow we will go on to consider in detail the nature and implications of the relationship between inflation and unemployment.

Part 2
The Phillips Curve

3 The Phillips Curve

Neoclassical economic theory had little to say about money wages and hence about the relationship between the rate of change of money wages and the level of unemployment. This was because the neoclassical theory of the labour market was couched in terms of real variables, and a clear dichotomy was drawn between real and monetary magnitudes. This dichotomy was attacked by Keynes in *The General Theory*,[1] and he himself attached considerable importance to the downwards rigidity of money wages. However, Keynes replaced the old dichotomy by the new when he went on to argue that a fundamental distinction needed to be drawn between states of under-employment and full employment respectively.

Keynes argued that money wages would remain more or less constant as the economy moved towards full employment from an initial position of under-employment under the stimulus of rising aggregate demand. At very low levels of unemployment, money wages would begin to rise slowly because bottlenecks would occur in the labour market (known as 'frictional' unemployment), but it was only once full employment was attained that money wages would suddenly rocket upwards. This would happen, he argued, because any further stimulus to demand in the labour market would simply cause employers to bid up money wages in an attempt to attract additional workers from other places of employment, given that the pool of previously unemployed labour had been wholly absorbed into the work-force. The above line of argument can be illustrated graphically as is shown in Figure 3.1.

Two points arising from Figure 3.1 merit further consideration. In the first place, it can be seen that as aggregate demand is decreased and the economy moves towards higher levels of unemployment, the fall in money wages which we would expect to accompany an excess supply of labour does not take place. In other words, money

FIG. 3.1

wages are sticky in a downwards direction, a phenomenon which was accounted for by Keynes by appeal to trade-union resistance to wage cuts. In the second place, it is clearly possible for the economy to operate at point *A* above where full employment is attained at virtually no cost in terms of wage inflation.

In the immediate post-war period the authorities were successful in their attempts to keep the economy at or near full employment through resort to Keynesian demand management. However, it soon became clear that money wages were not proving as predictable as was suggested by the above analysis, and especially that they tended to vary much more than they should have done in periods of under-employment. It was in response to this difficulty that econometricians began to devote increasing amounts of time during the 1950s to the study of the inflation–unemployment trade-off. The breakthrough came in 1958 when an article was published by Phillips[2] which, in the event, has stimulated what is possibly the largest volume of literature ever devoted to a single topic in the history of economics.

Since it is the quantitative aspect of the Phillips study which has engendered the most significant implications from the authorities' point of view it is convenient to begin our discussion by setting this out in the form of Table 3.1 and Figure 3.2.

TABLE 3.1 *Phillips Curve statistics, 1861–1913*

Unemployment Rate (U)	1·0	1·5	2·0	2·5	3·0
Rate of Change of Money Wages ($\dot{W}$)	8·7	4·6	2·8	1·8	1·2

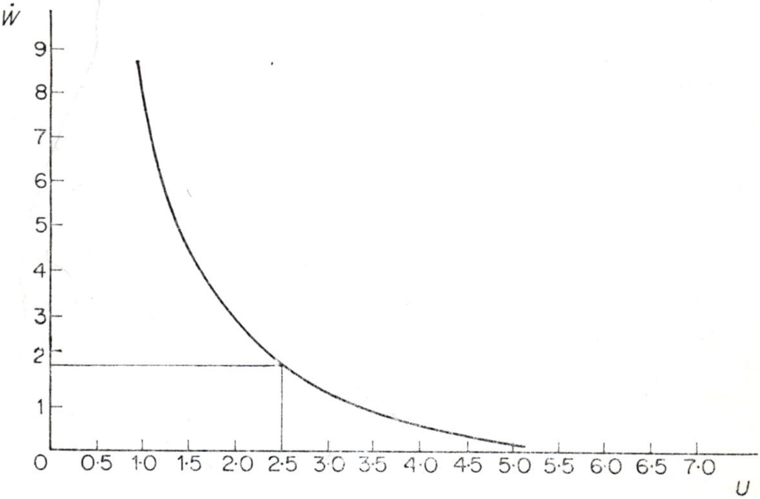

FIG. 3.2 *The Phillips Curve*

As can immediately be determined by inspection of Figure 3.2 the Phillips study threw up a curvi-linear relationship between unemployment and money-wage inflation which differed appreciably from its predecessors. This relationship is the true *Phillips Curve*, although, as we shall shortly discover, this term is now customarily used to describe the relationship between unemployment and *price* inflation. The Phillips Curve has several interesting properties. In the first place, it rules out of court any possibility of operating the economy at full employment combined with marginally positive rates of money-wage inflation. According to the Phillips Curve statistics, money-wage stability is only possible at a level of unemployment of approximately 5½ per cent. From a policy point of view a more relevant interpretation of the statistics is that if productivity is rising at 2 per cent per annum then at a level of unemployment of around 2½ per cent, price stability results, since the rate of change of money wages is then equal to the rate of change of productivity. Therefore, *provided that the Phillips Curve is taken at its face value* a fairly precise policy implication can be derived, namely that if the authorities are able to stabilise the unemployment level at around 2½ per cent, price stability will result. Furthermore, *provided that the Phillips Curve is taken at face value* it appears to offer the authorities a menu for policy choice as between a large number of inflation–unemployment combinations. Finally, and this is a matter on which we will have rather more to say a little later on, if it is accepted that the Phillips Curve illustrates a causal relationship such that changes in the level of unemployment *cause* subsequent changes in the rate of inflation, then the policy implication can be derived that *inflation can be controlled by increasing the pool of the unemployed.*

Now any reasonable interpretation of economic policy during the 1960s would indeed lead one to believe that the authorities did accept the Phillips Curve at face value, and that they did believe in the menu for policy choice which it offered. And it is precisely for this reason that we must give detailed consideration to the procedure adopted by Phillips in conducting his study, since it is now manifestly apparent that his work has been widely misinterpreted over the years.

The Phillips Study

In the course of his seminal article Phillips set out to apply to the labour market the standard supply and demand analysis used to explain the level of prices in the market for goods and services. In his own words[3]

> When the demand for labour is high and there are very few unemployed we would expect employers to bid wage rates up quite rapidly, each firm and each industry being continually tempted to offer a little above the prevailing rates to attract the most suitable labour from other firms and industries. On the other hand it appears that workers are reluctant to offer their services at less than the prevailing rates when the demand for labour is low and unemployment is high so that wage rates fall only slowly. The relation

between unemployment and the rate of change of wage rates is therefore likely to be highly non-linear.

Phillips's first point, therefore, was to argue the case for the use of data on unemployment as a proxy for the state of either excess demand or excess supply, as the case may be, in the labour market.

What Phillips then did was to plot annual figures for unemployment and for the rate of change of money wages over the period 1861–1913. The unemployment figure, *U*, was the average number of unemployed workers during the year in question, and wage rate change, $\dot{W}$, was also measured as an average during the year. This yielded 52 observations of each variable. Phillips found, however, that 'there were 6½ fairly regular trade cycles with an average period of about eight years'.[4] Each cycle is represented in broad outline by the cycle illustrated in Figure 3.3. The phenomenon shown in Figure 3.3 is generally referred to as the Phillips 'loop'. Its existence was explained by Phillips as follows:[5]

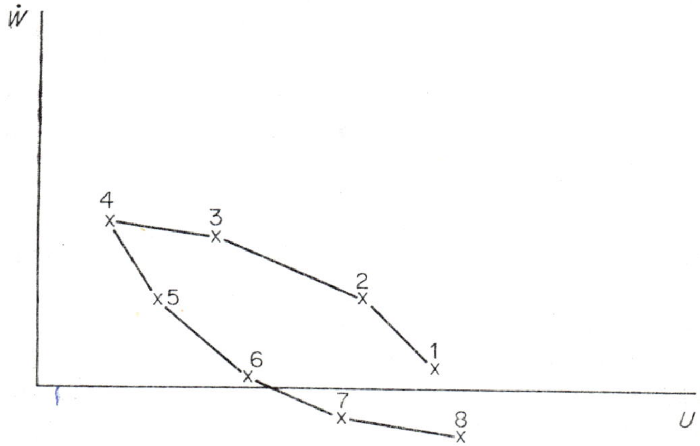

FIG. 3.3 *The Phillips 'loop'*

in a year of rising business activity with the demand for labour increasing and the percentage unemployment decreasing, employers will be bidding more vigorously for the services of labour than they would be in a year during which the average percentage unemployment was the same, but the demand for labour was not increasing. Conversely in a year of falling business activity, with the demand for labour decreasing and the percentage unemployment increasing, employers will be less inclined to grant wage increases, and workers will be in a weaker position to press for them than they would be in a year during which the average percentage unemployment was the same, but the demand for labour was not decreasing.

Phillips then proceeded to separate the observations of U into six ranges, namely 0–2 per cent; 2–3 per cent; 3–4 per cent; 4–5 per cent; 5–7 per cent; and 7–11 per cent. The next stage was to average out all of the observations of U and $\dot{W}$ which fell within each range so that he ended up with only six observations. Finally, he used regression analysis to obtain a line of best fit which had the property

$$\dot{W}+0{\cdot}9=9{\cdot}64\ U^{-1{\cdot}39}.$$

Phillips's justification for this unorthodox procedure was that[6]

> Since each interval includes years in which unemployment was increasing and years in which it was decreasing the effect of changing unemployment on the rate of change of wage rates tends to be cancelled out by this averaging, so that each cross gives an approximation to the rate of change of wages which would be associated with the indicated level of unemployment if unemployment were held constant at that level.

In other words, whereas the Phillips loop relates $\dot{W}$ both to U and to the rate of change of unemployment, $\dot{U}$, the grouping of observations has the effect of making $\dot{U}$ equal to zero at each point along the Phillips Curve.

This can be explained in one of two possible ways. Either Phillips wished to conduct his study in a time vacuum, a view put forward by Desai[7] who points out that the Phillips study contains no time subscripts; or the difficulties of computation could only be overcome by recourse to a two-variable equation, as is suggested by Phillips's own footnote to the effect that 'At first sight it might appear preferable to carry out a multiple regression of $\dot{W}$ on the variables U and $\dot{U}$. However, owing to the particular form of the relation between $\dot{W}$ and U in the present case it is not easy to find a suitable multiple regression equation.'[8]

In either event there are certain conclusions which lead on directly from the techniques used in the Phillips study. In the first place, no distinction can be drawn between a short-run Phillips Curve and a long-run Phillips Curve since, in Desai's words, 'In the short run it is hard to envisage $\dot{U}$ being kept equal to zero. Maintaining unemployment at a constant level implies a long-run equilibrium situation.' Hence, 'The Phillips Curve *is* a long-run Phillips Curve.'[9] Secondly, it becomes impossible to slide along the Phillips Curve in order to alter the terms of the inflation–unemployment trade-off because $\dot{U}=0$ at each point along it, and the act of moving along the curve necessarily requires that $\dot{U}$ be non-zero. Finally, the Phillips Curve cannot be used to predict the rate of change of money wages which will be associated with any given level of unemployment in a future time period because it is not a time-series relationship.

A couple of further points are worth making before we move on to examine subsequent studies. In the first place, although Phillips concentrated upon the relationship between U, $\dot{U}$ and $\dot{W}$ he also noted that[10] 'A third factor which may affect the rate of change of money wage rates is the rate of change of retail prices, operating through cost of living adjustments in wage rates.' He felt, however, 'that cost of living adjustments will have little or no effect on the rate of change of money wage rates except at times when retail prices are forced up by a very rapid rise in import prices'. In the second place it should be noted that Phillips took the curve which he had fitted to the 1861–1913 data and compared it with the scatter diagram of $\dot{W}$ and U for (a) the years 1913–48 and (b) the years 1948–57. Whereas the fit proved satisfactory for the former period, it can only be described as remarkably good for the latter period provided that unemployment is lagged by seven months. Thus at the end of the day Phillips found himself in the happy position of being able to present to the world that great rarity in the social sciences – a consistent causal relationship between two variables which had apparently lasted for a full century.

It is, however, extremely questionable whether the Phillips study should be taken at face value. His study has been widely criticised over the years, for the most part on highly technical grounds which cannot be dealt with in a book of this kind. Certain criticisms cannot, however, be overlooked. It is argued, for example, that Phillips did not employ either consistent or meaningful measures of either wage inflation or unemployment.[11] In the second place, it is argued that Phillips's explanation of the loops is unsatisfactory. And, in the third place, it is suggested that when Phillips's averaging procedure is applied to trade cycles post-1913 the relationships which transpire differ substantially from the pre-1913 Phillips Curve. This latter argument which is presented by Desai[12] is of particular interest because Phillips himself did not use his averaging procedure beyond 1913, but compared the curve based upon pre-1913 data with scatter diagrams for the two subsequent periods mentioned above. Desai's calculations produced five observations for the period 1914–47, and four for the period 1949–71. His conclusion was that '*The shape of the Phillips curve is not invariant from one period to another*.' Hence, 'Since the Phillips curve changes its shape in this fashion from one time period to another, the many attempts made to derive a single shape for the curve from an *a priori* theoretical consideration are futile.'

However, the acceptance of the Phillips Curve as a menu for policy choice had its origins not merely in the suspect Phillips study but also in a study by Lipsey which appeared shortly afterwards, and it is to this later work that we must now turn our attention.

The Lipsey Study

In his 1960 paper[13] Lipsey set out to reconsider Phillips's work in some detail. His first task was to duplicate the Phillips Curve using the ordinary-least-squares technique applied to Phillips's own observations. This he was able to do with a considerable degree of accuracy using the equation

$$\dot{W}=a+bU^{-1}+cU^{-2}+d\dot{U},$$

and setting $\dot{U}=0$ at all points. He then went on to query Phillips's contention that $\dot{U}$ was a variable whose importance was diminishing over time, and also analysed the role played by the rate of change of the cost of living index, $\dot{P}$. Lipsey's conclusion was that over the period 1862 to 1913 the Phillips Curve was best approximated by the equation[14]

$$\dot{W}=-1{\cdot}21+6{\cdot}45U^{-1}+2{\cdot}26U^{-2}-0{\cdot}019\dot{U}+0{\cdot}21\dot{P}.$$

This equation had an R^2 of 0·85 which means that 85 per cent of the variance in $\dot{W}$ was accounted for by variations in U, $\dot{U}$ and $\dot{P}$. It also had squared partial correlation coefficients of 0·78 for U, 0·50 for $\dot{U}$, and 0·17 for $\dot{P}$. These mean that variations in U explained 78 per cent of the variance in $\dot{W}$, that variations in $\dot{U}$ explained a further 50 per cent of the variance in $\dot{W}$ not accounted for by variations in U, and that variations in P explained a further 17 per cent of the variance in $\dot{W}$ not accounted for by variations in U and $\dot{U}$. Hence Lipsey's general conclusions that

(i) There is a significant relation between the rate of change of money wage rates on the one hand and the level of unemployment and its rate of change on the other. Over 80 per cent of the variance in money wage rates over the period 1862–1913 can be associated with these two variables U and $\dot{U}$.
(ii) The Phillips hypothesis that the influence of the rate of change of unemployment has diminished over the period is rejected.
(iii) The Phillips hypothesis that the cost of living enters with a threshold effect is rejected. There seems to be some evidence in favour of a simple (but rather weak) relation between changes in the cost of living and changes in money wage rates.[15]

Notice that Lipsey's equation contains four variables of which two are measured as rates of change. In other words, the Lipsey version of the Phillips Curve does not require the assumption of a time vacuum, and hence movements along the curve become possible should the authorities wish to alter the terms of the unemployment–inflation trade-off. Furthermore, it if is accepted that the association between unemployment and inflation is causal rather than coincidental, then it becomes possible to predict the rate of change of wages which will be associated with any given level of unemployment.

In the second part of his paper Lipsey set out to construct a theoretical model which would account for the observed relationship between $\dot{W}$, U and $\dot{U}$. He began by examining the behaviour of wages[16] in individual (micro) labour markets. The main characteristic of such a market was that labour was more mobile within it than between it and other labour markets. He argued first that the rate of change of wages in any one market was related to the excess demand for labour within that market, and, more specifically, that the greater the excess demand the faster would wage rates be changing. However, the condition of excess demand could result from shifts *either* in the supply curve *or* in the demand curve over time. Since excess demand for labour is not directly observable, he took the percentage of the labour force unemployed as a proxy for it. The relationship between the excess demand for labour and the level of unemployment appeared as an inverse non-linear relationship similar in shape to the Phillips Curve itself, principally because he assumed that zero excess demand must be accompanied by some positive amount of *frictional employment* – hence steadily rising excess demand must be accompanied by increasingly smaller reductions in unemployment. This relationship he combined with a proportional linear relationship between the excess demand for labour and the rate of change of wages, and the result was a micro market version of the Phillips Curve relationship between $\dot{w}$ and u (the small letters denoting variables in individual micro markets).

However, the above stage in the analysis referred only to micro labour markets, so that Lipsey's next task was to aggregate the various micro markets into a single macro market. Although the precise nature of the aggregation technique need not concern us here it should be noted that the aggregation process was affected not only by the rate of unemployment but also by its distribution amongst the various micro markets. More specifically, Lipsey argued that if the various micro Phillips Curves were identical then the macro Phillips Curve would be displaced above and to the right of the micro curves when unemployment rates were unequal as between the various micro markets.

In the final part of his theoretical analysis Lipsey turned to consider the Phillips loops. He observed that in order to obtain a loop it was necessary that something affect $\dot{W}$ without simultaneously affecting $\dot{U}$. Phillips had argued that this would occur because there would be more competitive bidding when $\dot{U}$ was negative than when it was positive, given that in the former case there would be net hiring of labour whereas in the latter case there would be net dismissals. Lipsey, however, preferred to interpret the loops 'not as positive and negative deviations from a stable macro relation between $\dot{W}$ and $\dot{U}$, but as upwards displacements from the stable single market relations between $\dot{w}$ and u,[17] the loops being produced by systematic variations in the degree of upward displacement'.[18]

He went on to illustrate the meaning of the above statement by following through the course of a hypothetical cycle in an economy with two imperfectly linked labour markets.[19] This appears as Figure 3.4 where the identical Phillips Curve for each micro market is illustrated by the broken line. The observed path of the aggregated

Phillips Curve during the course of a trade cycle is shown by the continuous line.

Now assume that the economy begins in a depression with excess supply in both micro markets, but with heavier unemployment in market *a* than in market *b*. Thus we have unemployment of 1*a* and 1*b* respectively which together yield observation I on the loop. Now assume that a recovery gets under way and that it is at first

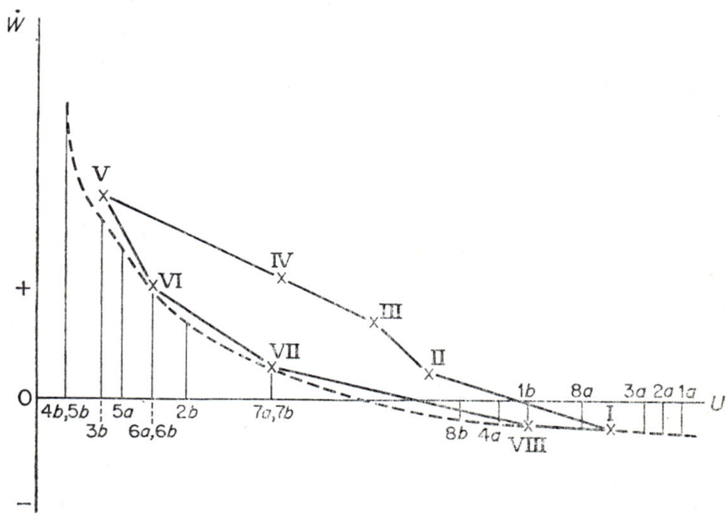

FIG. 3.4

mainly centred in market *b*. Unemployment in market *b* falls to 2*b* reflecting the pressure of excess demand which in turn drives up wages in that market. Meanwhile market *a* still suffers from excess supply and unemployment there remains at 2*a*. In periods 3 and 4 market *b* continues to suffer from excess demand and hence escalating wage levels. Meanwhile the excess supply in market *a* is gradually eliminated and it too begins to suffer from rising wage rates. The points on the loop numbered III and IV lie above and to the right of the micro curve because they reflect the *net* impact both of wages rising rapidly in one market but either slowly or not at all in the other, and of low unemployment in one market but high unemployment in the other. Clearly, therefore, throughout the upswing of the trade cycle the loop lies above and to the right of the micro curve.

The north-eastern bound of the loop occurs where unemployment in market *b* has ceased to fall and unemployment is only marginally heavier in market *a*. The trade cycle then moves into the depression phase and the points VI and VII on the loop are seen to fall along the micro curve. This is because Lipsey assumed that during the downswing unemployment would rise more or less uniformly in both markets. Over all, however, it is clear that the observations of $\dot{W}$ on the downswing lie well below those for corresponding levels of unemployment on the upswing, and hence the loop is explained. In Lipsey's own words 'the "loops" can thus be accounted for on the hypothesis that the recovery affects different markets at different times while the fall in effective demand is, at least during the early stage of the recession, more evenly distributed'.[20] He then went on to argue that

> if a relation $\dot{W}=f(U)$ were fitted to the macro observations of [Figure 3.4], the curve would go through the centre of the loop and thus be displaced upwards from the stable micro-adjustment functions. The observed macro-curve relating $\dot{W}$ and U goes through the centre of most of the 'loops' and therefore gives the average relation between $\dot{w}$ and u, *given the degrees of inequality in excess demand that have in fact been experienced.*

This can be expressed in another way by altering the Lipsey equation from $\dot{W}=f(U, \dot{U}, \dot{P})$ to $\dot{W}=f(U, q_u, \dot{P})$ where q_u is a measure of the inter-market dispersion of unemployment.

In the final part of his study Lipsey applied his four-variable equation based upon data covering the period 1862–1913 to data covering the period 1919–57. He found, however, that the inclusion of the war years and of the years 1920, 1921, 1922 and 1947 greatly biased the results, and that the exclusion of these latter years reduced the variance of $\dot{W}$ from 47·2 to 10·2. He therefore restricted himself to consideration of the periods 1923–39 and 1948–57. His most important conclusions were as follows:

(i) the changes in money-wage rates continued to be explained mainly by changes in U, $\dot{U}$ and $\dot{P}$.

(ii) however, the importance of $\dot{P}$ as an explanatory variable was considerably increased in the later periods as compared to the original period, the squared partial correlation coefficient rising from 0·17 to 0·76, and the regression coefficient in the Phillips

Curve equation rising from $0{\cdot}21\dot{P}$ to $0{\cdot}69\dot{P}$. In Lipsey's view this indicated a substantial movement in the direction of a one to one relation between changes in prices and changes in wages.

(iii) the two-variable Phillips Curve which related $\dot{W}$ to U with $\dot{U}=0$ had shifted between the original and later periods. The curve appeared to have pivoted about the 3 per cent unemployment level such that the curve covering the later periods lay above the original curve for levels of U greater than 3 per cent, but below the original curve for levels of U of less than 3 per cent.[21]

(iv) the equation for the curve fitted to the data for the years 1923–39 and 1948–57 was of the form

$$\dot{W}= +0{\cdot}74+0{\cdot}43U^{-1}+11{\cdot}18U^{-4}+0{\cdot}038\dot{U}+0{\cdot}69\dot{P}.$$

When compared to the equation fitted to the period 1862–1913 it can be seen that the regression coefficient for $\dot{U}$ had changed from negative to positive. This suggested that the Phillips loops had changed direction. However, further analysis showed that the direction effect applied to the 1920s and 1950s but not to the 1930s.

(v) the squared correlation coefficients for U and $\dot{U}$ had fallen from 0·78 to 0·38 and 0·50 to 0·30 respectively. These variables were therefore of considerably less importance in explaining the variance in $\dot{W}$ during the later periods as compared to the earliest.

Given the above factors Lipsey was drawn to the inevitable conclusion with respect to the Phillips study that '*although it might be held with a high degree of confidence that a significant and very interesting relation had been discovered, a very low degree of confidence might be attached at this stage to a particular estimate of the parameters*'.[22]

Further Developments

(i) What is the Phillips Curve?

The first question which must clearly be asked at this point is 'what is the Phillips Curve?' Now although this may appear superficially to be a rather odd question to ask after such a long discourse about the curve's origins, it should be borne in mind that we are interested in the Phillips Curve because of the policy implications which it provides. Two points are especially relevant in this context. There would appear to be little doubt about the fact that the authorities regarded the Phillips Curve during the 1960s as offering a menu for policy choice. For this to be so required, first, that they accepted the assumption that the relationship was causal, the direction of causality being from U to $\dot{W}$, and secondly that they assumed that it was possible to actually move along the curve in order to alter the terms of the trade-off.

Now there is no proof of causality in the Phillips study. What Phillips demonstrated was that there had been a consistently high degree of correlation between U and $\dot{W}$ over a hundred-year period. This relationship could, however, have been purely coincidental, arising perhaps from the nature of the trade cycle itself. Hence the existence of causality had to be explicitly assumed, the justification for this assumption being found in the unlikelihood of a non-causal relationship remaining in existence so consistently and over such a long period.

The assumption that it was possible to move along the Phillips Curve required that the variable $\dot{U}$ be non-zero. But as we have already noted the original Phillips-study equation contained only the two variables U and W and set $\dot{U}=0$ for all points along the curve. Thus it is manifestly obvious *that what is currently regarded as the Phillips Curve is not the curve which appeared in Phillips's own study*. In fact it bears a much closer resemblance to the Phillips Curve as postulated by Lipsey, and should perhaps in recognition of this fact more appropriately be called the 'Lipsey Curve'.

By now those readers familiar with introductory-level textbooks on economics will doubtless be wondering why the Phillips Curve has so far been regarded exclusively as a relationship between unemployment and the rate of change of *wages*. Surely the standard textbook model has on its vertical axis the rate of change of prices, $\dot{P}$? This is indeed correct, principally because the authorities are inclined to set rather more store by the statistics on price inflation than by those on wage inflation, which is only one constituent, albeit the most important one in many years, of price inflation. The variable $\dot{W}$ can be related to the variable $\dot{P}$ in a large number of ways. One possible model assumes that prices are determined by taking variable costs and adding to these a fixed percentage mark-up to cover costs and a margin for profit. Alternatively, the mark-up can be applied to the sum of fixed costs and variable costs. In his textbook[23] Lipsey himself assumes that all factor incomes increase at the same rate as wages and hence the point on the $\dot{W}$ axis equal to the contemporaneous rate of change of productivity then becomes the point on the $\dot{P}$ axis where $\dot{P}=0$. In other words, he uses the simplified relationship whereby the rate of change of money wages less the rate of change of productivity equals the rate of change of prices. The relationship between $\dot{W}$ and $\dot{P}$ tends to be rather more complex than this in practice, as we have seen in our previous discussion about why $\dot{W}$ and $\dot{P}$ are currently so far removed from one another. However, the choice of model for converting $\dot{W}$ into $\dot{P}$ does not affect the fundamental nature of the Phillips Curve and need not concern us any further at this point.

(ii) Studies post-Lipsey

During the past fifteen years an immense literature has appeared offering seemingly infinite variations on the theme of the Phillips Curve.[24] This literature has been concerned in particular either to alter the basic Lipsey equation through the addition of variables not considered by him, in order to improve the equation's predictive accuracy during the periods post-1913, or to redefine the Lipsey variables U and W with the same end in view. I do not propose to review this literature since this is done adequately elsewhere.[25] Besides which there is much to be said for Laidler's statement that in his judgement 'nothing of basic importance was added by this literature to the fundamental contributions of Phillips and Lipsey'.[26]

(iii) Cost-push versus demand-pull

Now it might well appear to the reader that we have made some significant progress in the analysis of inflation. Unfortunately this is so only up to a rather limited point. What we have demonstrated so far is that if the original Phillips equation is amended to include the variables $\dot{U}$ and $\dot{P}$ then a Phillips Curve appears which offers the authorities a menu for policy choice. But about the *causes* of inflation and about the *cures* for inflation we have so far learnt nothing at all except that if the authorities deflate the economy, thereby inducing higher unemployment, then the rate of inflation should diminish. (Inflation is henceforth *price* inflation unless otherwise specified.)

In order to discover what causes inflation we need to have a theory which *predicts both that a trade-off between inflation and unemploy-*

ment exists and that the terms of this trade-off can be adequately represented by the Phillips Curve equation. Now Phillips himself considered that changes in wage rates were induced by shifts in the *demand* curve of labour, but in his later study Lipsey argued that 'the observation of the postulated relation is quite consistent with changes in wages caused by union-induced shifts in the labour supply curve'.[27] Lipsey therefore concluded that it would be a serious mistake to try to judge between demand side and supply side causal factors on the basis of the evidence then available.[28]

During the early 1960s a considerable debate was conducted as to the causes of inflation. This rapidly became polarised into two opposing camps whose ideas have become enshrined in the literature as the 'cost-push' and 'demand-pull' theories of inflation.

The Demand-Pull Theory

The proponents of this theory held that the existence of excess demand for final goods and services would cause their prices to rise. Profits would improve as a consequence and hence firms would be induced to expand demand for the various factors of production which they employed. As a result the price of factors such as labour would themselves be bid up. Thus the theory argued that inflation would be sparked off by an excess demand for goods and services which would in turn lead, after a suitable time lag, to rising wages.

The demand-pull theory could be applied directly to the Phillips Curve by taking the level of employment as a suitable proxy for the state of excess demand. Rising excess demand, as proxied by falling unemployment, would lead to a speeding-up in the rate of price, and hence of wage inflation according to the logic of this theory, and the fact that the rate of inflation varied over time could be explained away by reference to variations in the level of excess demand.

The Cost-Push Theory

The proponents of this theory argued that inflation would be set off by exogenous increases in factor prices, and especially in the price of labour. Any increase in wages would, they argued, cause firms to raise the prices of final goods and services in an attempt to protect their profit levels. This would occur irrespective of whether or not excess demand for such goods and services was in existence at the time, although the extent to which firms would be able to pass on wage increases to the consumer would be partly determined by market conditions. Thus the theory argued that inflation would begin with rising wages which would hence precede the rise in prices of final goods and services, a direct reversal of the time sequence predicted by the proponents of the demand-pull theory.

But why should wages rise in the absence of excess demand for labour services? Essentially because, came the answer, of the ability of organised labour to press home wage claims even in unfavourable circumstances. Then why does the rate of wage inflation vary so much from one period to another? Because the pressure on employers to grant wage rises is linked to other factors. What factors are these? Well, trade-union-membership figures, for example, or industrial profitability (see Chapter 9). Then how does this produce a Phillips Curve? These other factors tend to be associated with the state of the economy. The more prosperous the economy the more obvious the opportunity for trade unions to try to exact higher wages from employers. The state of the economy can be proxied by the percentage of the work-force in employment. Hence the lower the level of unemployment the harder will trade unions press home wage demands and the higher will be the resultant rate of wage inflation and hence of price inflation.

It thus appeared during the early 1960s that variants of both the cost-push and demand-pull theories, in linking together causally the rate of inflation and the level of unemployment, could provide an adequate explanation for the existence of the Phillips Curve. Unfortunately, the obvious way out of this impasse, which was to determine whether wage rises preceded price rises or vice versa, proved too daunting a task, so that the adherents of the two theories were left to justify their opinions by recourse to further lines of argument. It was pointed out, for example, that an inflationary situation could hardly be set in motion without the prior existence of excess demand, because in its absence no employer could expect to be able to pass on any increased wage costs through higher prices without a resultant loss of profits when demand subsequently fell away. Wage claims would therefore be resisted strongly in the absence of excess demand even if a strike was threatened, and, even if they were eventually granted, employers would be forced to retaliate by laying off those workers deemed to be uneconomic at the new, higher wage levels. Individual employers could be expected to raise wages without simultaneously laying off workers only when they knew that price increases would not lead to an erosion of profits, and this would occur only if excess demand already existed for their products. Thus cost factors could not initiate an inflationary situation but could only perpetuate it.

'Not so' came the reply. In the first place, provided that all employers within the same industry were subjected to the same exogenous increase in wage costs, they could all simultaneously increase their prices without suffering any significant reduction in profits, other than where the over-all demand for the product was highly elastic, given that customers would be unable to switch suppliers in order to secure a price reduction. In the second place, the emphasis upon redundancies was no more than a red herring. Although redundancies would indeed occur if wage costs rose rapidly in the absence of excess demand, this would not affect the attitude of the unions to wage bargaining. The benefits of wage increases were immediate, whereas no one would be made redundant until some time had elapsed. Furthermore, a far greater number of workers would benefit from the wage rise than would suffer as the result of losing their jobs.

The cost-push versus demand-pull debate waged on through the 1960s to no great effect. In 1967, however, some apparently startling things began to happen to the Phillips Curve and the great debate of the 1960s rapidly got overtaken by events. It is with the period post-1967 that the rest of this book is concerned.

Part 3
Causes of the Current Inflation

4 Introduction to the Current Inflation

During the period 1958–66 the level of unemployment was associated with near enough the rate of change of wages predicted by the Phillips Curve, as can be seen by reference to Table 4.1. The period since 1967 has, however, been characterised by very high rates of inflation relative to the levels of unemployment sustained during these years. A wide range of explanations has been put forward

TABLE 4.1

	Unemployment rate	*Predicted changes in wage rates*	*Actual changes in wage rates*	*Prediction less actual*
1958	2·1	2·8	3·6	−1·1
1959	2·2	2·3	1·1	+1·2
1960	1·6	4·1	4·1	0
1961	1·5	4·6	3·4	+1·2
1962	2·0	2·8	4·4	−1·6
1963	2·5	1·8	4·3	−2·5
1964	1·6	4·1	3·8	+0·3
1965	1·4	5·2	4·6	+0·6
1966	1·5	4·6	3·3	+1·3
1967	2·4	1·9	5·9	−4·0
1968	2·4	1·9	7·1	−5·2
1969	2·4	1·9	5·7	−3·8
1970	2·6	1·6	13·5	−11·9
1971	3·6	0·7	12·1	−11·4
1972	3·7	0·6	11·0	−10·4
1973	2·6	1·5	12·2	−10·7

SOURCE: A. R. Prest and D. J. Coppock (eds), *The U.K. Economy. A Manual of Applied Economics*, p. 41.

concerning the apparent worsening of the unemployment–inflation trade-off since 1966. It is convenient to group these explanations into four general categories as set out below.

(1) There has not in fact been any worsening of the unemployment–inflation trade-off since 1966 despite appearances to the contrary. The illusion of a worsening trade-off stems not from the way in which the figures given in Table 4.1 are calculated but from employing the wrong definition of inflation and unemployment in the first place. If these terms are redefined to take account of changes which have occurred over the past decade, and new calculations done accordingly, the Phillips Curve reappears in more or less its old glory.

(2) The present inflation is simply a short-term aberration in relation to the customary long-term relationship between the level of unemployment and the rate of change of money wages indicated by the Phillips Curve statistics. Such aberrations have happened in the past but the customary relationship has always re-established itself. Thus there is every reason to expect that this will happen again, once the unusual forces responsible for the current inflation–unemployment trade-off have worked their way through the system.

(3) The basic causal association between the level of unemployment and the rate of change of money wages is not to be questioned. The Phillips Curve has, however, shifted bodily to the right, thereby associating a considerably higher degree of inflation with any given level of unemployment, and a considerably higher level of unemployment with any given rate of inflation. There is, however, no reason to expect the original Phillips Curve relationship to re-establish itself within the foreseeable future due to the emergence of new structural forces within the economy.

(4) The Phillips Curve is irrelevant because there is no causal association between unemployment and the rate of change of money wages. Therefore the best thing economists can do is to forget all about it and to produce a new set of policy measures based upon the way the economy really works.

Rehabilitation of the Phillips Curve

From the point of view of policy perhaps the most important distinction to be made between studies of the current inflation relates to whether or not they salvage the principle that a predictable amount of inflation is associated with any given level of unemployment. Provided the trade-off does still exist, and provided further that its magnitude can be predicted with reasonable accuracy, then the authorities do at least have something to go on. But if there is no longer a quantifiable trade-off then the authorities may be hazarding in the dark in their attempts to control the economy.

Taylor in particular[1] believes that the Phillips Curve retains its usefulness for policy purposes provided that greater care is taken in determining what is to be measured. In the studies conducted by Phillips and Lipsey the number of registered unemployed was used as a proxy for the excess supply of labour which is measured along the horizontal axis of the Phillips Curve. Taylor argues, however, that the excess labour supply consists not merely of the registered unemployed but, in addition, of both the hidden unemployed and labour that is hoarded. Hidden unemployment arises because secondary workers such as married women and retired men, who actively seek employment in a buoyant labour market, leave the labour force during recessions without registering at the employment exchanges. Labour hoarding refers to the under-utilisation of employed labour which can either be unpaid, for example where the availability of overtime working is drastically reduced, or paid for, for example where a firm retains its skilled work-force on full pay even though it cannot for the moment be gainfully employed.

But just as it is possible to prevent workers from putting in as many hours as they customarily wish to, it is also possible to induce workers to lengthen their usual working day. The point here is that the official unemployment level is obtained by counting the number of registered unemployed. An employer, however, is only interested in meeting any additional commitments on time, and this he can achieve either by taking on more workers, which will affect the official unemployment statistics, or by making his existing work-force put in longer hours, which will leave the official statistics unaffected. According to Taylor, employers typically preferred to meet increased demand prior to 1966 by taking on more workers, whereas they subsequently preferred to make the existing work-force put in longer hours, despite an increase in payments at overtime rates. This change in practice thus gave the impression that unemployment had risen noticeably whereas there had in fact been little change because it had not all been recorded in the official statistics before 1967.

Taylor therefore argues that labour hoarding diminished sharply after 1966. He suggests that this occurred first because, in spite of rising output levels during 1967–8, 'business expectations of future product demand were pessimistic in view of the continuing balance of payments crises facing the British economy during these years', and secondly because 'employers may simply have become more determined to raise labour productivity through a deliberate pre-determined shake-out'.[2]

Other explanations have been advanced to account for the increase in registered unemployment since 1966. Saunders,[3] for example, feels that 'the increased level of strike and industrial activity in the late 1960s may well have persuaded employers to attempt to minimise the size of their workforce'. Gujarati, on the other hand, emphasises the role played by *voluntary* unemployment, and goes on to suggest that the 1965 Redundancy Payments Act and the 1966 National Insurance Act enabled workers to spend more time searching for a job by increasing the amounts which they received while out of work.[4]

Some voluntarily unemployed workers may register as unemployed whereas others may not. An increase in voluntary unemployment should, however, show up as an increase in registered vacancies. Labour hoarding, on the other hand, does not show up in official statistics, so that if the period post-1966 was characterised by diminished labour hoarding, as Taylor suggests, we would expect to find a rise in registered unemployment as labour is shaken out combined with a fall in registered vacancies. This hypothesis is verified by the official statistics as shown in Table 1. 2 above (p.4).

Taylor also criticises the use of an index of weekly wage rates as a proxy for changes in the price of labour as measured on the vertical axis of the Phillips Curve. He considers that the basic wage rate is an under-estimate whereas average hourly earnings are an over-estimate because they include payment at overtime rates. He therefore employs as a proxy for the price of labour the rate of change in average hourly earnings corrected for overtime.[5]

Having thus redefined the axes of the Phillips Curve to read 'rate of change in average hourly earnings corrected for overtime' on the vertical axis, and 'rate of registered wholly unemployed plus rate of labour hoarding' on the horizontal axis, Taylor proceeds to plot the relationship between wage inflation and unemployment between 1954 and 1970.[6] He concludes that, whereas a trade-off between wage inflation and registered unemployment as defined by Phillips does not exist, a consistent trade-off can still be detected using his special proxy variables. Hence, in his opinion the Phillips Curve has not disappeared.

5 The Role of Money

The analysis of the current inflation is fairly notable for the controversies which it has engendered, although it has been suggested that a meeting between two economists always produces three points of view! The greatest controversy of them all,[1] however, relates to the role played by money in the propagation of inflation. This is now referred to almost universally as the 'money-supply controversy'. As we shall go on to see below, this controversy has its roots in neoclassical economics and also encompasses both Keynes's own work and post-Keynesian writings. In order to avoid confusion it is convenient to group together those writers whose approach to the role of money has its foundations in *The General Theory* under the umbrella title of 'Keynesians' (or 'neo-Keynesians', or 'post-Keynesians'), although it should be clearly understood that we cannot, by so doing, do proper justice to the full range of their ideas.[2] The strict Keynesian approach to the money-supply controversy can be summed up in the dictum 'money does not matter'. For our purposes, however, the Keynesian view can more appropriately be expressed as 'money is not all that matters'. The contrary view in this controversy is associated with a school of thought known as the 'Monetarists' or 'New Quantity Theorists', whose chief advocate is Professor Milton Friedman of the University of Chicago. The strict Monetarist approach can be expressed as 'money is all that matters'. Most Monetarists, however, subscribe to the looser version that 'money is not all that matters but is considerably more important than anything else'.

In so far as both Keynesians and Monetarists apparently assign some role to money in the propagation of inflation it may appear superficially that the money-supply controversy is a storm in an academic teacup. However, this is far from the truth in practice, as the sections which follow will make clear, since there is a fundamental divergence between the policy prescriptions advocated by the respective schools of thought.

The Quantity Theory of Money

It is necessary to begin our discussion of the role of money by outlining one of the major foundation stones of neoclassical economics, known as the *Quantity Theory of Money*.

The Quantity Theory was originally formulated in order to provide a theoretical rationale for the observed tendency for prices to rise at times when the quantity of money was rising at a faster rate than the production of goods and services. In its original, unsophisticated, form the Quantity Theory said that the quantity of money and the general price level were proportionately related, or in other words, that a one per cent increase in the money supply would result in a one per cent increase in the price level.

The Quantity Theory incorporated a demand for money function defined solely in *transactions* terms. Households were held to need money in order to transact purchases of goods and services, as did firms which also needed money in order to pay wages. It therefore followed that the transactions demand for money was linked proportionately to the level of National Income since if, for example, all incomes doubled, exactly twice as much money would be needed in order to pay people for their labour services.

The Quantity Theory then went on to argue that if households and firms had more money than they required for current transactions purposes, they would spend the excess on further purchases of goods and services. In other words, they would hold no assets in the form of cash balances. Now any attempt to dispose of surplus cash by buying up goods and services could, in principle, have one of two possible effects. Either it could lead, in the presence of unemployed resources, to an expansion of output at current prices, or, in an economy already working at full capacity, it could lead to the same amount being sold but at higher prices. But given the neoclassical emphasis upon full employment as the equilibrium condition of the economy, to which it would automatically revert (through an adjustment in relative prices)[3] despite periodic disturbances, the former alternative could only be a short-run phenomenon. In the longer run any increase in the supply of money would have no impact upon output but would permeate through directly to the price level.

The Quantity Theory is set up formally as follows. The first thing to consider is the *value of transactions* within the economy. This can be re-expressed as the amount of money which is handed over in exchange for goods and services, and is composed of (i) the number of transactions per time period, T; and (ii) the average value per transaction, P.

In addition we need to take into account the money supply, M, and a concept known as the *velocity of circulation*, V, which is the average number of times that any currency unit is employed in order to effect a transaction during the time period in question. Thus where the money supply, M, is £1 million, and the value of transactions, PT, is £10 million, then each currency unit must on average be used 10 times in order for the value of transactions to be 10 times as large as the stock of money.

The Quantity Theorists combined the above four variables into the equation, $MV=PT$.[4] On the left-hand side of this equation is the total amount of money given up in order to pay for goods and services, MV, whereas on the right-hand side of the equation is the value of goods sold, PT.[5] The two sides of the equation are thus directly equivalent to one another since the value of what is sold cannot help but be equal to the value of the money stock given up in exchange.

But if MV and PT are merely two different ways of expressing the same magnitude then the *equality* $MV=PT$[6] is more appropriately expressed as the *identity* $MV\equiv PT$.[7] So is not the Quantity Theory a tautology, and what information, if any, does it yield? In fact all that the Quantity Theory can tell us when expressed as an identity is the value of V which is otherwise difficult to estimate, given that M, P and T are measured statistically by the authorities.

However, the Quantity Theory took on a different meaning when interpreted in the light of the neoclassical view of how the economy worked. As already mentioned the neoclassical school regarded the economy as being in a state of equilibrium only when output was sufficient to require the employment of everyone who wished to work. Where, however, output was for any reason insufficient to induce full employment then changes in the relative prices of factors of production would automatically restore equilibrium. In terms of the Quantity Theory equation this made T a constant (equal to the full-employment level of transactions) apart from the occasional minor (self-adjusting) fluctuation.[8]

Neoclassical economists also assumed that V would be a constant over time.[9] In other words they believed that households and firms would always keep a constant percentage of the value of transactions in the form of cash balances. Hence they would respond to a doubling of prices by doubling their demand for money to hold for transactions purposes.

But if V and T were constants then only M and P were left free to vary. Therefore the equation $MV=PT$ could only be satisfied by a *fixed proportionate relationship* between M and P. Thus, to sum up, the neoclassical school turned what was originally simply an identity, serving no purpose other than to measure V, into an equation which hypothesised a proportionate relationship between the money supply and the price level by the expedient of holding both V and T constant. But a crucial proposition contained within the Quantity Theory was that the *direction of causality* was explicitly from M to P. In effect, the Quantity Theorists were arguing that the price level was dependent primarily upon the money supply, changes in which would *cause* the price level to change by the same proportion and in the same direction.

However, the Quantity Theory did *not* imply that the money supply could be manipulated by the authorities as a major instrument of stabilisation policy. In the first place, the currency unit at the time was a gold coin[10] and the supply of gold was determined largely outside the jurisdiction of the U.K. authorities, whose control over the money supply was as a consequence extremely limited. In the second place, manipulating the money supply would simply cause the price level to vary up and down but would have no direct impact upon real variables such as output and employment. If the economy was suffering from temporary unemployment then the neoclassical school held that this was caused by an excess supply of labour which remained in existence because workers were unwilling to lower the price of their services relative to those of machine time. Their policy prescription was therefore a general cut in wages[11] rather than an increase in the money supply.

Keynes and Money

Although the *Treatise on Money*[12] marked a major step forward in Keynes's ideas about the role of money in the economy, it is to *The General Theory*[13] that we must turn to find the concepts which are fundamental to post-Keynesian writings. At the heart of Keynes's analysis of what he called the 'money market' is a respecified demand for money function.

Keynes began by arguing that the demand for money was not associated solely with a desire to conduct transactions. Two further motives for holding money could be identified. The first of these he called the *precautionary* motive on the grounds that cash is often needed to cover unforeseen contingencies. Cash reserves can also be used to make an unforeseen advantageous purchase although, clearly, there are risks involved in running down precautionary balances. Such balances are therefore tied to the level of National Income because as National Income rises so, similarly, precautionary balances need to rise in order to offer a constant level of protection against the possibility of running out of cash. They are also tied more loosely to the cost (as measured by the rate of interest) and the availability of short-term credit, which might be needed if things go wrong after precautionary balances have been run down.

Keynes also identified a *speculative* motive for holding cash balances. He pointed out that firms or households with spare cash can, if they so wish, invest it in a number of ways. In particular they tend to invest in fixed-interest securities, called *bonds,* because they do not wish to undertake the risks of equity investment.

Now the rate of interest and the real value of a bond are inversely related. This can be shown by the fact that a yield of £10 can be obtained either from a £100 bond yielding 10 per cent or from a £50 bond yielding 20 per cent. Thus a rise in interest rates will be accompanied by a fall in the market value of bonds, and vice versa.

Now where bond prices are historically low, and interest correspondingly high, it is doubly advantageous to invest any spare cash in bonds, first because they are cheap, and secondly because they have a high yield. Conversely, where bond prices are historically high, and interest rates correspondingly low, it is doubly advantageous to hold cash rather than bonds, first because bonds are costly, and secondly because their yield is poor. Each individual who is considering whether to hold cash or bonds for speculative purposes must give some thought to the direction in which he expects interest rates to move. If a speculator expects interest rates to fall, he should buy bonds in order to make a capital gain. Hence, if interest rates are usually high, then we would expect speculators to hold no cash for speculative purposes. On the other hand, where interest rates are unusually low, we would expect speculators to hold cash in the expectation of rising interest rates. Finally, where interest rates are hovering around what appears on past experience to be their customary level, we would expect some speculators to take a chance on falling interest rates, and hence to hold bonds whereas others will prefer to hold cash. All of these possibilities can be conveniently illustrated by what Keynes called his *liquidity-preference function* (shown in Figure 5.1).

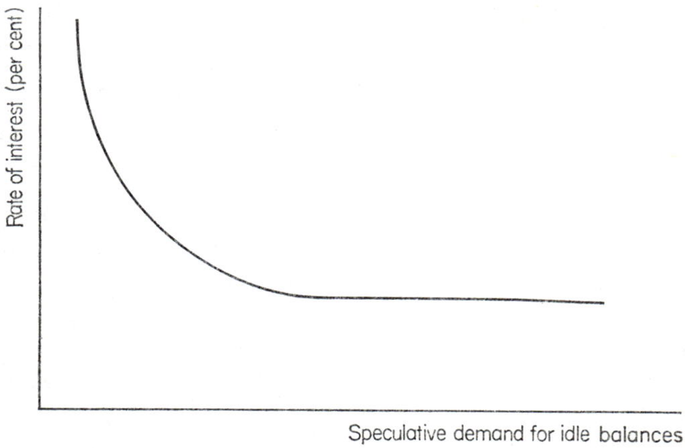

FIG. 5.1 *The liquidity-preference function*

Note that there is a horizontal section along the lower end of the liquidity-preference function. This is known as the *liquidity trap* and effectively describes a situation in which interest rates have fallen so low relative to their customary levels that no one wishes to hold bonds because there is a universally held belief that interest rates must subsequently rise.

Now in describing the workings of the money market we have already come across the Quantity Theory formula, $MV = PT$, where the demand for money was expressed purely in terms of transactions balances. It is a matter of convenience at this juncture to express this formula as $MV=PY$, where PY stands for the level of *money* National Income.[14] You will remember that the neoclassical system operated only in the context of a fully employed economy, in the sense that anyone who wanted to work at the going wage rate would be employed. The Keynesian model, however, expressly introduced the possibility of *involuntary* unemployment such that an increase in the money supply would initially affect real National Income, Y, beyond which point it would affect the price level, P, with Y remaining unchanged.

Since we are mainly concerned at this juncture with an exploration of the effects of changing the money supply we can usefully re-express the above formula as $M=\frac{1}{V}PY$. This formula, however, allows only for a demand for money function expressed in terms of transactions balances. In order to incorporate the Keynesian speculative demand for money function the formula needs to be extended through the addition of an expression which shows the influence of the interest rate. This yields the Keynesian formula $M=\frac{1}{V}PY+L^2(r)$ where r represents the interest rate.

Now consider what will happen if the money supply is increased when the interest rate is initially above that ruling in the liquidity trap. This leaves speculators holding additional idle balances which some of them will choose to retain in the form of cash holdings whereas others will choose to exchange the cash for bonds in the money market. As explained above, the choice between strategies will reflect differing views as to the probable future course of interest rates. Provided, however, that some speculators do attempt to buy additional bonds at the prevailing interest rate then this will push up the price at which bonds are being offered for sale and push down the interest rate which they yield accordingly.

But, as the interest rate falls, so progressively fewer speculators will find it an attractive proposition to buy additional bonds rather than to hold cash, and there must, by implication, be some interest rate which will bring about a new equilibrium between the increased supply of money and the demand for money to hold for speculative purposes. This movement towards equilibrium is represented by a movement down the liquidity preference function in Figure 5.1.

The fall in the interest rate will in its turn make investment and consumption expenditure a more attractive proposition than it was previously, and there will be an eventual impact upon the level of National Income (henceforth to be regarded as a *real* variable unless otherwise qualified). Thus there is a link in the Keynesian system between the money supply and economic activity. This link was, however, regarded by Keynes as being rather weak. He believed first that unless interest rates were initially very high relative to their customary level, then changes in the supply of money would cause no more than a negligible movement in interest rates. Furthermore, he felt that investment spending was anyway very volatile and also interest-inelastic, as was consumption spending, which is to say that they would respond very little to small changes in the prevailing interest rate because such changes would do nothing much to alter the state of expectations about the future.

In terms of the above Keynesian formula what we are saying is that changes in the money supply lead principally to changes in the interest rate, and only indirectly to changes in PY. But in order for the two sides of the formula to remain in balance when M increases much faster than PY, it is necessary for *V to diminish in size*. Now you will remember that the Quantity Theory operated on the assumption that V was a *constant*, thus producing a proportionate relationship between the money supply and the price level. Hence Keynes's demonstration that V varied inversely with changes in the money supply brought to light an apparently fatal flaw in the logic of the Quantity Theory.

This can be made more explicit if we consider what will happen if the money supply is increased when the liquidity trap is in operation, although the liquidity trap is itself best regarded as an exceptional case which has had little relevance in the post-war world. Figure 5.1 above shows clearly that the whole of any increase in the money supply will be absorbed into idle balances with no resultant impact upon the interest rate. But if the interest rate remains unchanged there can be no subsequent change in the level of investment and consumption expenditure nor, hence, in National Income. In terms of the Keynesian formula what we are saying is that M is bigger but Y is unchanged. For this to occur, there must clearly be a falling-off in the income velocity of circulation, V, sufficient to counterbalance exactly the rise in M. That this should happen is hardly surprising in view of the fact that idle balances do not circulate at all, so that the average velocity of circulation must diminish as idle balances are built up. Since, however, the constancy of V is integral to the Quantity Theory, its validity is destroyed when the liquidity trap is in operation.

Fiscal Policy

Now we have noted in the course of our analysis of Keynes's views on money that, although Keynes did assign some importance to increases in the money supply as a means of stimulating growth in National Income, or, as it is more popularly known, in Gross National Product (G.N.P.), he expected the relationship to be weak and unpredictable. It is for this reason that the Keynesian stance in the money-supply controversy can best be expressed as 'money is by no means all that matters', although money does not matter at all in the liquidity-trap position. This being so it is appropriate to outline at this point the essential elements in Keynesian anti-inflationary policy.[15]

Fundamental to the Keynesian model is the assertion that the level of aggregate demand, and hence of output and employment, is determined on the one hand by consumption decisions taken by households, and on the other hand by investment decisions taken by businessmen.[16] Keynes argued that any change in future expectations would cause households to amend their savings out of income by adjusting their precautionary cash balances, and would cause businessmen to amend their investment plans. The initial impact of either action would then be adjusted in turn by the *expenditure multiplier* which measures the relationship between an initial change in expenditure and its eventual, much enlarged, impact upon National Income. Now in Keynes's opinion the result of such actions taken independently by households and by businessmen could be destabilising, unlike the neoclassical model, where, as we have seen above, full employment was restored automatically. As expectations change so the response of the private sector might well either drive output down below its full-employment level, or might cause prices to rise where the economy is already working at full capacity. In view of this, Keynes advocated the need for government intervention designed to iron out such fluctuations in expenditure with the over-all objective of ensuring just enough expenditure to maintain the full-employment level of output.

In the specific context of an economy suffering from excessive private demand resulting in upwards pressures upon prices, Keynesian analysis proposes that inflation can be controlled either through changes in the amount, composition or timing of government expenditures, or through variations in the burden, structure or frequency of tax payments. More specifically the government can

(1) reduce household disposable income either by increasing direct or indirect taxation – by decreasing transfer incomes (money given away by the government in the form of pensions, unemployment benefit, family allowances, subsidies, and so on); or by increased borrowing from the private sector via, for example, National Savings;
(2) decrease investment either in the public sector (for example spending either by local authorities or by nationalised industries on capital projects), or in the private sector (for example by increasing corporate taxation or by reducing investment allowances and other forms of subsidy);
(3) decrease government expenditures either by providing fewer free services (for example health and education services), or by reducing public works of all kinds (for example road building).

Any of the above measures can be introduced in isolation. It has become customary, however, to introduce whole packages of fiscal measures simultaneously in the form of a *Budget*, since no single measure can be expected to have much restraining effect upon prices unless carried to excess.

The New Monetarism

During the early post-war years the United Kingdom firmly embraced Keynesian doctrines and looked to fiscal policy as the principal instrument for controlling the economy. Unfortunately, as we have already indicated, the authorities proved unable to maintain full employment without running into periodic balance-of-payments crises, nor could they prevent continued mild inflation. In May 1957 the decision was taken to set up a Committee whose purpose was to investigate the working of the monetary system in order to determine whether monetary instruments should be given more prominence in the pursuit of economic stabilisation. The Committee, headed by Lord Radcliffe, reported in 1959.[17] The *Report*'s main conclusion was that monetary instruments would be of little use for purposes of short-term demand management other than in 'emergencies', and very little faith was placed in the stabilisation potential of changes in the money supply.

In the United States, however, the 1950s saw the emergence of a major new school of thought under the leadership of Professor Milton Friedman. Commencing in 1956[18] he and his disciples[19] propounded the view that the money supply was the all-important monetary aggregate on which the monetary authorities would have to concentrate their attention if they wished to have any meaningful control over economic activity. According to the volumes of data thrown up by their research there was a clear relationship between the long-run trend line of money National Income and that of the money supply. This relationship can be illustrated by a simple graph as in Figure 5.2 (which is not, however, drawn to scale).

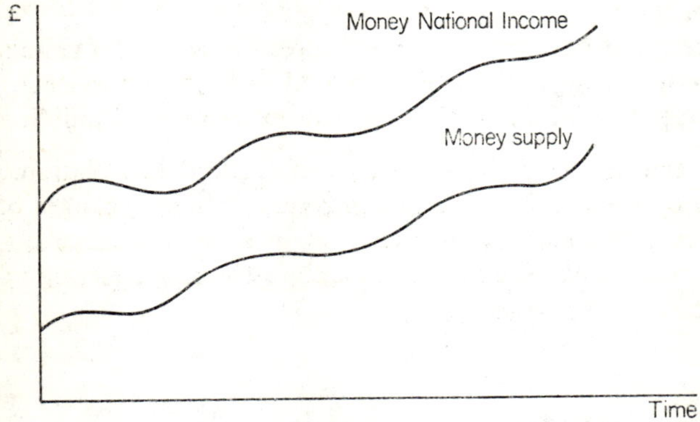

FIG 5.2

Although Friedman's data went back beyond the turn of the twentieth century the most significant ingredient of the historical retrospect linking *M* and *PY* was his assertion that the role of monetary policy during the Great Depression had been widely misunderstood. Keynes and his disciples believed that the U.S. monetary authorities had pursued aggressively expansionary monetary policies during the period 1929–33 but that these policies had proved ineffectual. Friedman, however, contended that the U.S. monetary authorities had pursued highly *deflationary* policies. According to his research the quantity of money in the United States fell by one-third during the course of the Depression, thus providing clear evidence that monetary policy was extremely *effective* in regulating the level of economic activity rather than the reverse.

Once armed with this high statistical correlation between the money supply and money National Income in the long run, Friedman went on to argue that the direction of causation was from M to PY, although the response of PY to changes in M would be lagged rather than instantaneous. Upon this foundation he then constructed a modern version of the Quantity Theory of Money which made some concessions to the earlier Keynesian theory of money, without, however, incorporating either any allowance for instability caused by the existence of a speculative demand for money or a liquidity trap.

One of the most important innovations of the New Quantity Theorists was to introduce an alternative demand for money function. Friedman argued that money should be regarded as one of five main ways of holding wealth, the other four being bonds, equities, physical goods (such as property), and human wealth.[20] He then moved one step away from the old Quantity Theory which had assumed V to be a constant, by arguing that significant changes in any of the above variables would cause V to vary. On the other hand, he saw no reason to expect V to vary much in the short term although a gradual long-term movement was to be expected. He contrasted the relative constancy of V in the short term, and its steady (and hence predictable) alteration over time, with the volatility of the money supply, and concluded that M and V could be treated as existing independently of one another. This being so, changes in money National Income could be traced almost exclusively to changes in the money supply.

The main strand in the New Quantity Theory was therefore that the money supply provided the all-important monetary determinant of the level of money National Income. Furthermore, the empirical data appeared to the Monetarists to suggest that, in the long term, the money supply influenced the level of money National Income in a predictable way, such that the achievement of steady long-term growth in money National Income could only be achieved through adherence to steady long-term growth in the money supply. On the other hand, it also appeared to suggest that the effects of varying monetary measures in order to deal with short-term problems would be unpredictable, largely because of the time lags involved, and that such measures were therefore best avoided. Discretionary[21] monetary policy of the traditional kind was, accordingly, deemed to be inferior to the steady long-run growth in the money supply as a means of promoting economic growth without inflation.

This preference for long-run rather than short-run monetary measures has become known as the *money-supply rule*. In essence, the policy prescription of the Monetarists is that the money supply, suitably defined, should grow at a steady and regular rate, month in and month out, thus providing both a stable monetary background for short-run adjustments and also a significant force for economic stability in the longer term. The growth path chosen for the money supply should be equated with the projected growth path of productivity in order that any increase in output should be accompanied by a roughly equivalent increase in the amount of money available to buy it. Expressed in terms of the New Quantity Theory, $MV=PY$, where V is broadly constant in the short term, the implication is that M and Y increase by equivalent amounts then there can be no need for any upwards adjustment in the price level.

The Money-Supply Controversy in Perspective

The above analysis begs a large number of questions,[22] some of which we must try to answer before we can draw any really valid conclusions about the money-supply rule as an instrument to be used in the control of inflation. First, we must question the direction of causality between the money supply and money National Income. Secondly, we must enquire whether the money supply can be measured at all accurately, since the authorities can hardly control to good effect an instrument the existence of which is ill-defined. Thirdly, we must consider whether the empirical evidence does lend adequate support to the hypothesised link between the money supply and inflation. Finally, we must consider in the light of the answers to the above questions whether we would be better to stick to discretionary rather than inflexible policies, and, if so, whether the emphasis should be placed upon monetary or fiscal instruments.

(i) The direction of causality

Statistical evidence of a high correlation between the money supply and money National Income does not of itself demonstrate the direction of causality. Monetarists believe that changes in the money supply *cause* changes in economic activity.[23] Keynesians, on the other hand, argue that what has happened in the past is that the authorities have tended to alter the money supply in order to bring it into line with changes in *PY which have already taken place*.[24] The Monetarists, in their turn, do not dispute that this may have happened on occasion but, on the other hand, they feel sure that were the authorities to alter the money supply with the specific intention of affecting *PY* then this policy would prove successful. To this the Keynesians respond that there have been too few occasions in the past on which the authorities have used changes in the money supply as a major policy instrument to give real substance to this argument, and that such occasions have, anyway, met with little success. That this is true should come as no surprise according to the Keynesians, since they contend that there are many other factors which can affect the level of economic activity quite independently of changes in the money supply, such as variations in private or public investment, in government expenditure, or in exports and imports. Hence they contend that the close relationship between *M* and *PY* is unlikely to last long once such independent forces have had the opportunity to exert their influence.

There are no simple answers to the question of the direction of causality. Ideally one would recommend to the reader that he examine carefully the link between the money supply and economic activity as set out in empirical studies, but this is too ambiguous, at least so far as the United Kingdom is concerned, to provide much assistance in this matter. However, it may be that the matter can be settled by recourse to other lines of argument.

(ii) The definition of the money supply

In order to demonstrate a causal relationship between changes in the money supply and changes in economic activity one must clearly adopt a widely acceptable and consistent definition of terms. There are, however, many possible combinations of financial assets which can be used for the purpose of defining the money supply.[25] The Bank of England currently publishes two sets of data known as M_1 and M_3,[26] as well as figures for Domestic Credit Expansion. Data on these three aggregates covering the recent five-year period appear in Table 5.1.

TABLE 5.1 *Money-stock changes (£ millions)*

Changes in period	M_1			M_3			Domestic credit expansion
	Unadjusted	Seasonally adjusted	(per cent)	Unadjusted	Seasonally adjusted	(per cent)	Unadjusted
1970 1st qtr	−300	+15	+0·1	−430	+110	+0·7	−944
2nd qtr	+346	+339	+3·9	+733	+567	+3·5	+711
3rd qtr	+179	+106	+1·2	+387	+446	+2·6	+483
4th qtr	+605	+340	+3·7	+896	+443	+2·5	+794
1971 1st qtr	+58	+378	+4·0	+15	+569	+3·2	−586
2nd qtr	+141	+125	+1·3	+471	+300	+1·6	+262
3rd qtr	+381	+325	+3·3	+452	+504	+2·7	+296
4th qtr	+475	+207	+2·0	+1428	+1012	+5·3	+1171
1972 1st qtr	+80	+363	+3·3	+460	+960	+4·7	+520
2nd qtr	+508	+488	+4·3	+1698	+1539	+7·1	+2373
3rd qtr	+201	+173	+1·5	+955	+1061	+4·6	+1191
4th qtr	+728	+479	+4·0	+2186	+1739	+7·2	+2794
1973 1st qtr	−323	−36	−0·3	+894	+1485	+5·7	+917
2nd qtr	+846	+832	+6·7	+1528	+1294	+4·7	+1675
3rd qtr	−293	−342	−2·6	+2329	+2333	+8·1	+2691
4th qtr	+423	+272	+2·1	+2462	+2144	+6·9	+3350
1974 1st qtr	−530	−354	−2·7	+463	+1041	+3·1	+718
2nd qtr	+403	+426	+3·3	+946	+637	+1·9	+1927
3rd qtr	+333	+346	+2·6	+829	+1099	+3·2	+1423
4th qtr	+1226	+997	+7·4	+1953	+1372	+3·8	+3241

SOURCE: *Bank of England Quarterly Bulletin* (Mar 1975).

M_1 consists of notes and coins in circulation plus sterling current accounts of the U.K. private sector held with the banking sector. M_3 incorporates both the above monies and also deposit accounts, accounts denominated in foreign currencies, and deposits owned by the public sector. M_3 is therefore a broader aggregate than M_1 and is roughly akin to the concept of 'liquidity' since it includes assets which can be quickly converted into cash. However, neither definition includes the sterling deposits of overseas residents nor is any indication given of unused bank-advance facilities (because of lack of accurate data) which are an obvious candidate for inclusion in any aggregate which is concerned with potential spending power.

Domestic Credit Expansion (D.C.E.) combines the growth in the domestic money supply with the surplus or deficit on the balance of payments.[27] The inclusion of D.C.E. figures in the money accounts reflects the view that inflationary pressures can manifest themselves through the running of balance-of-payments deficits. In 1974, for example, the figures for M_1 and M_3 suggested that the authorities were pursuing a tight monetary policy. However D.C.E. was growing at a much faster pace because of the huge current-account deficit on the balance of payments. On the other hand, in 1971 D.C.E. grew much more slowly than M_3 because, at that time, there was a massive inflow of 'hot' money hedging against a revaluation of the pound.

If we examine more or less any period over the past decade we will find a significant discrepancy between the growth rates for M_1, and M_3 and D.C.E.

In the third quarter of 1973, for example, the differential growth rate between M_1 and M_3 was over 10 per cent, and that between M_1 and D.C.E. was larger still. Monetarists contend that the precise definition of the money supply does not greatly affect the results.[28] However, the various formulations of the money supply are not equally proficient indicators of future money National Income. M_3, for example, suffers from an exclusion of deposits held with trustee savings banks and of share and deposit accounts held with Building Societies, since these are treated by many depositors in much the same way as bank deposit accounts. Some commentators favour D.C.E. as the best indicator 'of the stance of monetary policy at times when the current balance of payments is in big surplus or deficit'.[29] However, there is widespread agreement about the difficulties of defining the money supply in such a way as to provide a really satisfactory indicator, and there is also some controversy about the degree of control possessed by the authorities over the various money-supply measures.[30]

(iii) A survey of the evidence

With the above qualifications in mind we can now turn to consider whether the empirical evidence supports the contention that the money supply is the all-important monetary aggregate. Unfortunately, as is so often true, the bulk of the available evidence relates to the United States, and there are certain dangers in too readily accepting the proposition that if the case is proven for the United States then it is also proven for the United Kingdom.[31] I therefore propose to outline below only those few studies which use U.K. data.

One prominent study was conducted, not surprisingly, by Friedman himself. He correlated the quantity of money (using the M_2 definition) and Net National Product (N.N.P.) for the United Kingdom between 1880 and 1969,[32] and found that over those nine decades the money supply grew twenty-fivefold and N.N.P. grew twenty-sixfold. He concluded that it was impossible for anyone to overlook such similar movements in two completely independent series, and that the direction of causality was from the money supply to N.N.P.

A prominent U.K. monetarist, A. A. Walters, estimated that over the period 1877–1939 a one per cent increase in the money supply was associated with a one per cent increase in the level of money National Income, although the relationship between the two magnitudes had become more complex since the mid-1950s.[33] The simultaneous introduction of fiscal and monetary measures by the authorities made it difficult to pinpoint the effects of each measure taken individually. On the whole, however, Walters believed that 'even in the (monetarily) chaotic post-war years the statistics suggested that the money stock had an effect which was independent of budgetary (and other) policy'.[34] Hence 'one of the main general implications is that the Government should stabilise the quantity of money'.[35]

Most other studies have proved far less conclusive.[36] Bain has summarised a good deal of evidence relating to the United Kingdom, the United States and other countries.[37] His own opinion is that 'this controversy has certainly not demonstrated the superiority of "monetary" over "Keynesian" models of the economy. . . . But equally, the controversy has not demonstrated that monetary factors are unimportant.'

(iv) Rules versus discretion

Now all of the preceding discussion is fundamentally important with respect to the control of inflation. We have outlined above the conflicting Keynesian and Monetarist views of what causes a change in money National Income. In the former case, the central mechanism is the Keynesian 'expenditure multiplier' which primarily associates changes in consumption or investment with output, employment and prices, and, in the latter case, it is the analogous 'money multiplier' which associates changes in the money supply with changes in money National Income. But upon which variables should the authorities act in order to control inflation, and what is the time scale within which anti-inflationary policies can be expected to operate?

The first alternative is clearly to curb the rate of growth of the money supply, and preferably to hold it in line with the projected growth trend in productivity. Now adherence to this money-supply rule implies belief in the essential stability of the economy. The Monetarists hold that major business-cycle movements that have occurred in the past can be attributed primarily to large swings in the rate of growth of the money supply, and that further, for reasons outlined below, attempts at discretionary monetary and fiscal policy have tended to make things worse rather than better.

It is important, however, to bear in mind that the relationship between the money supply and money National Income is itself lagged. Friedman has expressed this as follows:[38]

> Studies for the United States and many other countries reveal highly consistent patterns. A substantial change in the rate of monetary growth which is sustained for more than a few months tends to be followed some six or nine months later by a change in the same direction in the rate of growth of total dollar spending. To begin with, most of the change in spending is reflected in output and employment. Typically, though not always, it takes another year to eighteen months before the change in monetary growth is reflected in prices. On the average therefore it takes something like two years for a higher or lower rate of monetary growth to be reflected in a higher or lower rate of inflation.

In other words, it is the belief of Monetarists that the current rate of inflation is the direct and inevitable consequence of changes in the money supply which took place some two years ago, and hence, by implication, curbing the rate of growth of the money supply cannot be expected to reduce inflation in the short term.

Most commentators are reluctant to adopt the rigid money-supply rule. In many cases they argue that no mechanical rule can be relied upon at all times.[39] Certainly this appears to be the view held by the Bank of England. As the Deputy Governor has remarked the difficulties of defining, measuring and interpreting the money supply are so substantial that 'while the money supply does really matter, they have to be faced and largely overcome before we can put more than limited weight upon any particular measure of money supply as a practical guide to policy in the sense of enabling us to judge what may be taken as the "appropriate" amount of money to suit a particular set of economic circumstances'. Hence 'what I am certain about is that there are limits to what – in the real world – can be achieved by monetary policy alone'.[40]

This reluctance to adopt a money-supply rule is accounted for, at least in part, by the technical shortcomings of those studies which purport to demonstrate the superior performance of a money-supply rule.[41] More important, however, are the practical policy considerations of introducing such a rule.[42] Of particular importance in this respect is the *Debt-management constraint*. Now the monetary authorities in the United Kingdom have traditionally been able to control either the money supply (through open-market operations, funding, the Special Deposits scheme and the issuing of directives) or interest rates (through operations in the gilt-edged market). In selecting its optimal strategy the Bank of England has, however, been greatly constrained by its role as manager of the National Debt.[43] In this capacity the Bank has been, and to a lesser extent still is, concerned with maximising demand for Treasury Bills and gilt-edged stocks by limiting the scope of downwards movements in their prices, both to provide finance for current government expenditure and also to ensure that new securities are sold to replace those reaching maturity. In addition, however, because of the high servicing costs on outstanding debt, the Bank has always felt the need to stabilise interest rates at a level which minimises the burden of these charges.

As a market operator, however, the Bank has rarely been able to dictate both the quantity of Debt taken up by the private sector and also its purchase price. In other words, the Bank could either fix the quantity on offer and accept whatever price it could get for it, or it could fix the price and let the market determine how much would be taken up. Traditionally the Bank invariably opted for control over interest rates in preference to control over the money supply. The reasons for this are rather complex,[44] but one consideration was, for example, the desire to lengthen the maturity structure of the Debt in order to avoid the need to refinance excessive amounts of maturing short-term debt.

However, although small fluctuations in interest rates were generally considered unobjectionable, close control over the interest-rate structure meant that the demand for securities was rarely in equilibrium with their supply, and hence, by implication, that the Bank was greatly constrained in its ability to manipulate the cash and liquidity ratios of the commercial banks in order to regulate the money supply. Attempts by the Bank of England to constrain credit expansion by reducing the liquid assets held by the commercial banks were also frequently frustrated by the willingness of the secondary banking system to provide commercial banks with fresh liquid assets as and when the need arose.

Clearly, therefore, adherence to a money-supply rule would imply much greater fluctuations in interest rates than has been customary. The authorities have in fact made some moves in this direction in more recent history, partly as a result of international pressure. In May 1969 the Chancellor of the Exchequer stated in a Letter of Intent to the International Monetary Fund that the authorities would set a specific quantitative target for Domestic Credit Expansion, and this was reaffirmed in a statement made by the Governor of the Bank of England in May 1971. It has been suggested, however, that this was no more than a sop to the growing influence of U.K. Monetarists.[45] In the event the monetary reforms heralded in by the document entitled 'Competition and Credit Control',[46] which came into force in September 1971, have made comparatively little impact upon the money supply. As can clearly be seen in Table 5.1 (p. 58) the authorities have not in general been prepared to allow interest rates to rise to the great heights needed to bring about a significant reduction in the money supply, whatever definition of the latter is used.

For reasons which will become clear in the course of the subsequent chapter on the international aspects of inflation, adherence to a money-supply rule would also require floating rather than fixed exchange rates. Other requirements are a greater willingness to allow fluctuations in the level of unemployment and stricter curbs upon the growth of public-sector spending.[47] What all this amounts to in a nutshell is that it is one thing to argue that the authorities are technically capable of controlling the money supply in adherence to a money-supply rule, but quite another to suggest that this can be done without recourse to possibly significant changes in institutional arrangements. As the authorities have so far eschewed reliance upon anything remotely akin to a money-supply rule there is, however, no real way of knowing precisely what would be involved.

But if adherence to a money-supply rule appears less than satisfactory, is salvation to be found in discretionary policies, whether fiscal or monetary? The Monetarists think not because they see such policies working pro-cyclically rather than counter-cyclically for reasons set out below. On the other hand, exactly the same argument has been levelled at the money-supply rule.[48] It is therefore appropriate to enquire at this point just what time lags are involved in the operation of discretionary monetary and fiscal policy.

There is now a considerable literature on this subject.[49] The trouble is that there is little unanimity of opinion about the length of lags. The estimated lags range from about four months to about two years whether we consider fiscal or monetary policy. The higher estimates are rather disturbing. The objective of discretionary policies is to get them to take effect in inverse relation to the trade cycle, that is to extract spending power in inflationary booms. Obviously, such policies need to be set in motion well in advance of when they are expected to take effect, depending upon the estimated time lags in question. But if the time lag associated with any given measure is subject to a good deal of uncertainty, then this makes it difficult to estimate the optimal moment for its introduction. In addition, it may well appear perverse to the authorities to introduce deflationary measures when economic activity has clearly not yet reached its peak.

Yet delays may prove disastrous. A deflationary fiscal or monetary measure which takes over a year to work to full effect may bear fruit at a time when the economy has moved into the downturn of its own accord. The measure will then serve to aggravate rather than to mitigate the approaching depression. Unfortunately, the likelihood of this occurrence has been increased by the apparent shortening of the trade cycle over the past two decades.[50]

It is also difficult to distinguish between the relative efficacy of fiscal and monetary measures by examining testing procedures other than the measurement of the relative length of time lags, basically because the empirical evidence is lacking for the United Kingdom. We have to remember in this respect that there have been no significant periods during which the economy has been controlled exclusively by either fiscal or monetary measures. Hence most of the arguments tend to be conducted in the abstract. We have already noted the main prongs of the Keynesians' denigration of monetary policy, namely those concerning the direction of causality, the demand for money function and the definition of the money supply, so it is perhaps appropriate at this point to clarify the Monetarist attitude towards discretionary fiscal policy.

But before we begin one further matter warrants our attention with respect to interest rates. In the Keynesian model, monetary policy is presumed to be useful only to the extent that higher interest rates and credit rationing have the effect of curbing aggregate demand. Hence high interest rates are regarded as a sign of monetary stringency rather than monetary ease. Monetarists, however, contend that increases in the money supply only result in falling interest rates in the short term. Once full recognition is taken of the likely upwards impact of extra money upon the rate of inflation, prospective holders of securities will insist on being paid a higher rate of interest by way of compensation. Hence, from the monetarist viewpoint, high interest rates reflect monetary *ease* rather than the reverse. But the Monetarists anyway regard the interest-rate issue as something of a trumped-up charge. Unlike Keynesians they do not see changes in the money supply working indirectly via induced changes in interest rates and hence in investment. Rather they see the link between the money supply and money National Income as being essentially direct, although they have not as yet brought forth any widely accepted explanation of the precise transmission mechanism.

Not only do the Monetarists pour scorn upon the Keynesian interpretation of the role of money, but they also belittle the efficacy of fiscal measures except in so far as they affect the government's net borrowing requirement. Monetarists assert that, whereas the Keynesian expenditure multiplier may be positive in the short run, in the long run it will be zero in the absence of accommodative monetary action. This results from what is often referred to as the 'crowding-out' effect. It is argued that if there is no accompanying increase in the money stock, government expenditure must be financed either by taxes or by borrowing from the public. In either case command over resources is simply transferred from the private sector to the government with little over-all impact upon *total* spending and hence upon output and employment. Only if the government finances its increased expenditure by creating money, the Monetarists argue, can there be any real impact upon aggregate demand. Hence, by implication, it is the monetary variable rather than the fiscal variable which influences economic activity.[51]

In conclusion it must be admitted that the role played by money in the inflationary process is still very much a matter of controversy. Neither Monetarists nor Keynesians have as yet been able to provide any really conclusive evidence to support their positions, nor are the theoretical issues exactly crystal clear. That this has serious implications from a policy viewpoint is manifestly clear since the two schools of thought are in disagreement with each other's remedies. We shall have more to say about this problem when we come to consider possible solutions to the current inflation in the latter part of this book. In the meantime it is our next task to incorporate the role of expectations into the foregoing analysis.

6 The Role of Expectations

The problem of inflationary expectations did not figure in the early studies of the Phillips Curve. More recently, however, two contrasting views on the causes of inflation have become widespread. The first of these, to which detailed reference will be made in Chapter 8 entitled 'The Role of the Trade Unons', holds that the current inflation is caused by forces which were largely absent from the economy during the early 1960s. The second view, on the other hand, holds that the only thing which has changed significantly of late is the expectation of inflation held by employers and workers alike. This view is closely associated with the Monetarists, and it merits careful consideration at this juncture because it has significant implications with respect to the control of inflation. The literature on expectations is vast[1] and grows at an acclerating rate. In this chapter, therefore, I propose to limit myself to a non-technical consideration of how expectations of the future rate of inflation are formed, and of how changes in such expectations can set off an inflationary spiral.

The Measurement of Expectations

One difficulty which immediately arises when any attempt is being made to assess the role played by changing expectations in the propagation of inflation is how such expectations are to be measured. Most of the early studies used data on past rates of actual inflation in order to generate estimates of expected inflation, but this exercise proved unsatisfactory.[2] Turnovsky and Wachter[3] were the first to compile an independent series on the expected rate of inflation. Their basic data came from the *Philadelphia Bulletin* whose financial editor, J. A. Livingstone, conducted a biannual survey of business economists which required them to predict for periods of six months ahead and twelve months ahead respectively the expected change in various price and wage indices.[4] However, this survey is of limited value because it is a poor guide to expectations of the future rate of inflation held by the population as a whole.

More recently Carlson and Parkin[5] have calculated a quantitative measure of the expected inflation rate based upon a Gallup Poll survey of approximately 1000 people in Great Britain selected on a stratified quota basis. Every month since July 1960 these people have been asked to assign the expected trend in prices into one of four categories, namely 'go up'; 'go down'; 'stay the same'; and 'don't know'. Carlson and Parkin then evolved a complex econometric technique which when applied to the interviewees' answers resulted in an expected inflation series which, in broad terms, corresponded well to the actual inflation rate.

The Formation of Expectations

Assuming for the moment that expectations can be measured accurately by the above technique we must now turn to consider why they are prone to fluctuate, often quite significantly, from one time period to another. The most obvious candidate in this respect is prior experience of actual inflation which can be explained by two mechanisms, known as extrapolative and error-learning (or *adaptive*) mechanisms respectively.

(i) Extrapolative expectations

One version of this hypothesis is supplied by Turnovsky[6] whose basic equation asserts that 'the expected price change for the next six months equals that for the past six months together with a correction needed to allow for the trend in price changes over the past six months'. He concluded that this performed rather better than error-learning mechanisms for the United States, but this does not appear to be the case for the United Kingdom in the light of the performance of an extrapolative mechanism tested by Carlson and Parkin.[7]

(ii) Error-learning mechanisms

A simple and popular error-learning mechanism holds that expectations of future inflation adjust in proportion to the last recorded error,[8] that is the extent to which expectations in the current period differ from those in the previous period depends upon the margin of error between the expected and actual rates of inflation during the previous period. Carlson and Parkin also test a more sophisticated mechanism which takes account of both the recent rate of inflation and its rate of change. This they express first in the postulate that people adapt to the size of their previous two errors, and secondly in the alternative postulate that the change in expectations depends upon the size of the last error and the change in the last error.[9]

Carlson and Parkin conclude that 'comparing alternative error-learning and extrapolative schemes, a second-order expectations scheme is, ignoring the possible influence of other variables, the best simple characterisation of the formation of expectations of inflation'.[10]

(iii) Other variables

Carlson and Parkin go on to test the influence of other variables upon inflationary expectations. These include (1) certain variables which might affect actual inflation, and hence a rational person's expectation of it, namely (*a*) changes in the foreign exchange rate, and (*b*) changes in the political party in power; and (2) variables which it lies within the power of the government to control with a view to altering expectations, namely (*c*) wage–price controls/guidelines (or norms), (*d*) voluntary price restraint, (*e*) large and highly publicised wage increases, and (*f*) changes in indirect taxes.

Carlson and Parkin conclude that whereas the Confederation of British Industry voluntary price restraint in 1971 may have contributed to a downwards adjustment of expectations, the only really significant variable was the exchange rate. Their best estimate is that the 1967 devaluation, to which we will return in the following chapter, raised the expected inflation rate by 6 per cent at an annual rate.[11] Their considered view is, however, that expectations are primarily determined by a stable second-order error-learning process.

As they then go on to point out this conclusion has somewhat unfortunate policy implications in so far that it implies that the only way to reduce inflationary expectations is through a reduction in the actual rate of inflation itself. Manipulation of the variables labelled (*c*)–(*f*) above is unlikely to prove of any lasting value in this respect, although revaluation of the currency should prove of some assistance.

The Expectations-Augmented Phillips Curve

Money illusion has an important role to play in the process through which changing expectations affect the rate of inflation. The essence of the argument is that, during the early post-war years, workers measured the improvement in their standard of living by the rate at which their *money wages* grew in value. Once, however, prices began to rise more rapidly during the late 1960s, and it became clear that this was a continuing trend; workers began to sense that their standard of living was not in fact improving at the desired rate. As a result money illusion, which had previously been widespread, ceased to hold sway and workers began to negotiate for increases in their *real wages*.

Let us suppose, for illustrative purposes, that the desired real-wage target is 5 per cent p.a.; that money wages are rising at 5 per cent p.a.; productivity at 3 per cent p.a.; and prices at 2 per cent p.a. The actual rise in real wages is therefore 3 per cent p.a. Workers come to realise, however, that their standard of living is not improving at the desired rate, and take note of the fact that actual prices are rising by 2 per cent as compared to their previous expectation that prices would be stable. The error-learning mechanism comes into play and wage claims are adjusted upwards by 1½ per cent, which is some proportion of the previous error. In other words they expect prices to be 1½ per cent higher in the subsequent bargaining period. Now faced by a wage demand for a 6½ per cent rise firms must make one of three choices; either to turn the claim down and risk a strike; to raise prices by a further 1½ per cent in order to keep profits constant; or to raise prices by a lesser amount and permit some redistribution out of profits into wages. In all probability employers will initially regard concession of the wage claim in full as being preferable to a strike, especially as they will probably be in a position to raise prices by 3½ per cent without becoming uncompetitive. But workers expect prices to rise by only 1½ per cent and their real-wage aspirations are frustrated as a consequence. So next time around they put in for a rise of 8 per cent since, taking into account their previous two errors, they now expect prices to rise by 3 per cent over the forthcoming bargaining period.

This time around we assume that employers cannot pass on the whole of the increase through higher prices because their competitive situation is less secure, so they put prices up by 4½ per cent and permit some redistribution out of profits into real wages, which go up by 3½ per cent. But workers expected prices to rise by only 3 per cent so once again they raise their wage claim, this time to 9½ per cent, and so it goes on. In this example real wages are measured before tax. The effect of the tax system is, of course, to widen the differential between a worker's desired improvement in his standard of living and that which he achieves in practice.

The above sequence can usefully be summarised as is shown in Table 6.1. This illustrates a fairly smooth path towards an equilibrium situation in which workers achieve their desired rise in real wages of 5 per cent. The path towards equilibrium can, however, be radically disturbed by, for example, a devaluation of the currency. The 1967 devaluation, as already mentioned, caused a sharp upwards movement in price expectations which meant that, in the short term, workers once again found themselves falling well short of their target growth rate of real income. This set off the process described above all over again, only this time all the variable values were at correspondingly higher levels. In view of this it is fairly easy to see how the rate of both wage and price inflation can rapidly escalate to unprecedented heights.

TABLE 6.1 *Frustrated expectations and the escalation of money-wage claims*

Period	Change in money wages (per cent p.a.)	Change in productivity (per cent p.a.)	Change in prices (per cent p.a.)	Change in real wages (per cent p.a.)
1	5	3	2	3
2	6½	3	3½	3
3	8	3	4½	3½
4	9½	3	5½	4
5	10½	3	6	4½

Now the above analysis has potentially significant implications when applied to the Phillips Curve. We have already noted the propositions which underly the Curve, namely that the equilibrium wage rate is determined by the forces of supply and demand in the labour market,[12] and that the rate of change of wages is determined by the degree of either excess demand or supply for labour which exists at any particular point in time. But the Phillips Curve illustrates the relationship between the rate of change of *money* wages and the excess demand for labour, as proxied by the level of unemployment. This is not, however, the same thing as an inverse relationship between the rate of change of *real* wages and the level of unemployment, except in conditions of price stability. Yet we have already argued that workers bargain for *real* wages (irrespective of whether money illusion does or does not exist), so the Phillips Curve clearly needs to be amended in order to allow for the possibility that prices are rising over time if it is to tell us anything useful about the trade-off between inflation and unemployment.

The necessary adjustment can be made by taking account of *price expectations* rather than of current prices. This is because workers make allowances for the difference between money and real wages by reference to *future* prices and not to current prices, as explained above. Now if we accept that any given level of unemployment is compatible with a single equilibrium rate of change of *real* wages, and that as unemployment falls the equilibrium rate of real-wage inflation rises, it becomes clear that each level of unemployment can have associated with it any number of possible rates of *money-wage* inflation. In other words, workers add to their desired improvement in real wages the amount by which they expect prices to rise during the ensuing period covered by the wage bargain. But this amount is purely arbitrary, and there is no reason to suppose that each time that the unemployment level reaches a particular level workers will expect an identical rise in prices to transpire as existed the last time that that particular unemployment level was attained.

We can think of the above argument in terms of a family of Phillips Curves as is shown in Figure 6.1. In this figure curve (*a*) represents the Phillips Curve when prices are stable. If, however, prices are expected to rise by 2 per cent then the Phillips Curve shifts up to become curve (*b*). In other words, each level of unemployment is associated with a rate of change of money wages 2 per cent higher than before. Likewise each level of unemployment is associated with a rate of change of money wages 4 per cent higher than before along curve (*c*) where prices are expected to rise by 4 per cent.

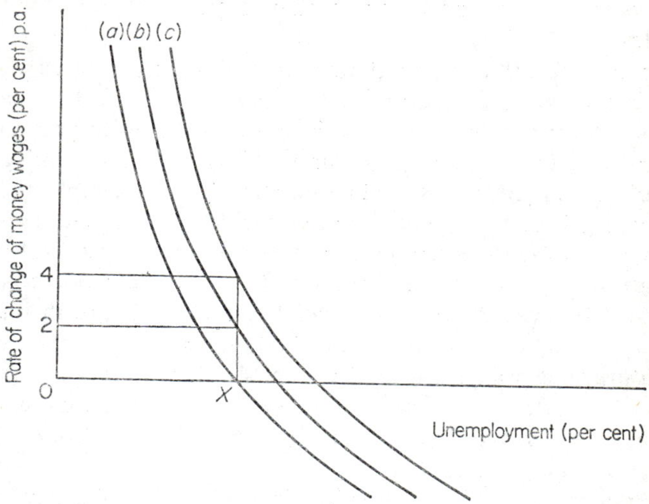

FIG. 6.1

Now the above clearly demonstrates that the Phillips Curve can only be a transitory phenomenon in so far as it purports to illustrate a trade-off between unemployment and *money*-wage inflation. This is because even if the unemployment level is stationary over a considerable period of time the rate of money-wage inflation will rise consequent upon upwards adjustments in price expectations, and the Phillips Curve will shift upwards as illustrated in Figure 6.1.

One issue which is, however, subject to some controversy is whether or not a trade-off between money-wage inflation and unemployment exists *in the long run*. Two possibilities exist in this respect. Either a long-run trade-off exists, but this trade-off is on considerably worse terms than in the short run,[13] or there is no trade-off at all in the long run.[14] This latter proposition is based upon the argument that in the long run inflation becomes fully anticipated. In other words the path towards equilibrium as illustated in Table 6.1 above eventually produces a rate of change of money wages which exceeds the actual rate of change of prices less the rate of change of productivity by an amount equal to the desired rate of change of real wages. Expected prices and actual prices then become one and the same.

Once inflation is fully anticipated both wages and prices rise thereafter at a constant rate, although this rate can vary freely in accordance both with differences in the rate of wage inflation at the time when expectations began to change and with the time taken to restore equilibrium.

It is argued further that inflation can only be fully anticipated at what is known as the *natural rate of unemployment*. This natural rate is determined by factors such as the availability and cost of labour-market information, labour mobility, and the relative cost and efficacy of job seeking while employed and unemployed.[15] In other words it is that rate of inflation at which there is neither excess supply or nor excess demand for labour as a whole. This equilibrium or 'natural' unemployment level is almost certainly not constant over time because those factors which determine it are themselves subject to variation. Irrespective of whether or not it varies, however, the natural unemployment level is compatible with *any steady rate of inflation*, for reasons explained above. In the long run, therefore, fully anticipated inflation is analogous to a *vertical Phillips Curve* as depicted in Figure 6.2.

The policy implications of the long-run vertical Phillips Curve are extremely serious, since it very clearly implies that there is no long-run trade-off between inflation and unemployment. But consider further what will happen if the government attempts to lower the level of unemployment below the natural rate. This will initially cause a movement up the short-run Phillips Curve, which will in

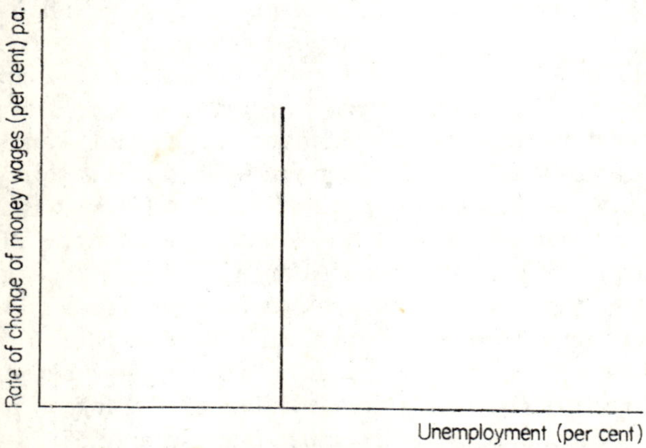

FIG. 6.2 *The vertical long-run Phillips Curve*

turn set off an expectations-induced spiral of rising wages and prices. Furthermore, if the level of unemployment is kept *persistently* below the natural rate then equilibrium cannot be restored and inflation will grow at an ever faster rate.[16]

By way of summary we may note that the expectations-augmented Phillips Curve hypothesises that wage inflation is determined primarily by variations in excess demand and in expectations about the future course of prices. In the long run, persistent excess demand for labour may set off a never-ending acceleration in the rate of inflation. However, even if the trade-off between inflation and unemployment does not disappear entirely in the long run, the terms of the trade-off are far less advantageous in the long run than in the short run. Adherents of this approach to the analysis of inflation argue that excess demand has its domestic origins in two sources in particular, namely Budget deficits, and increases in the money supply originating elsewhere. They also hold, however, that excess demand can originate in the external sector, and it is for this reason that we must turn to consider in the chapter which follows the role played by the balance of payments. Before we do so, however, there is one further question which warrants our consideration.

Expectations and Taxation

It is sometimes argued that the 1970 wages explosion was caused by trade-union frustration in the face of the decline in the growth of real disposable income *per capita* caused by tax changes during the six-year period prior to 1969. The effects of changes in direct taxation can be seen in Table 6.2.

TABLE 6.2 *Rates of growth in gross money, real and net real income, men manual workers (per cent p.a.)*

	Gross money income (*a*)	Gross real income (*b*)	Net real income (*c*)	Price effect (*a*−*b*)	Tax effect (*b*−*c*)
1948–52	6·9	0·6	0·7	6·3	−0·1
1952–6	7·2	3·6	3·5	3·6	0·1
1956–60	5·0	2·9	2·1	2·1	0·8
1960–4	5·5	2·2	1·3	3·3	0·9
1964–8	6·6	2·5	0·5	4·1	2·0
1968–70	10·0	3·6	1·3	6·4	2·3

SOURCE: F. Wilkinson and H. A. Turner in *Do Trade Unions Cause Inflation?* ed. Jackson, Turner and Wilkinson, p. 66.

Increases in indirect taxes contribute towards the price effect, and it is certainly true that indirect taxes were raised considerably during the period 1967–9.[17] Equally it is true that deductions by way of direct taxation, incorporating National Insurance contributions, rose appreciably during the latter half of the 1960s. What is at issue, however, is whether or not trade unionists sought to reverse this downwards trend in the growth of real disposable income by putting in for greatly inflated money-wage claims in 1970. According to the Midland Bank 'the experience of the five or six years up to 1969 seems to suggest that attempting to treat the consumer as the residual claimant on the resources which he produces may generate an inflationary backlash as he tries to offset a dwindling share by stepping up the growth which he seeks in his money income'.[18]

Parkin, Sumner and Ward[19] do not, however, accept this hypothesis. In their model they argue that the supply of labour depends upon the real wage which is 'the ratio of the money wage net of all taxes to an average price of consumer goods gross of all indirect taxes (and net of subsidies)', whereas the demand for labour 'depends upon the ratio of the gross cost of labour (the wage rate gross of direct taxes plus employers' social security taxes) to the net price of output received by firms'.[20] According to their calculations expectations were not affected by changes in direct taxation.[21] Indeed if anything wage demands appeared to be reduced in response to rising proportions of income deducted at source. Higher rates of indirect taxation are assumed to affect expectations of future prices since they contribute directly to changes in the Retail Price Index. They feel, however, that such changes did not in general affect expectations significantly since wage-earners did not expect indirect taxes to be raised for the purposes of inflation control. In view of these findings they see no reason to amend their version of the expectations–augmented Phillips Curve to take any further account of tax changes.

In a more recent study Bruce[22] set out to test the hypothesis that the rate of change of money-wage rates in Canada had been significantly influenced by changes in the average rate of income taxation plus the incidence of government wage deductions for unemployment insurance during the period 1953–70. He investigated five industrial sectors using annual data and the ordinary-least-squares technique in order to establish the relationship between the percentage rate of increase of money-wage rates and (1) the absolute change in taxes and deductions for unemployment insurance contributions expressed as a percentage of wage incomes in industry during the previous year; (2) the current level of profits in each industry as a percentage of labour costs in that industry; (3) the percentage increase in the money value of sales by industry during the current year; (4) the number of workers unemployed in the economy as a percentage of the aggregate labour force during the current year; and (5) the percentage increase in the consumer price index during the previous year.

Bruce's main conclusion was that 'significant and positive correlations exist between changes in wage deductions and changes in money wages in three of the five industrial sectors considered; and that evidence of a similar relationship is indicated in a fourth sector.'[23] An over-all view of the studies cited above leads us to conclude, therefore, that the evidence on the relationship between tax changes and money-wage claims during the 1960s is both limited and contradictory. Furthermore, these studies have nothing to say about how wage claims are affected by expectations of future Budget measures. This is by no means surprising since the 1960s were not characterised by a stream of crisis Budgets such as that which has poured forth over the past two years. Given the present economic climate, however, the assumption must surely be that if tax changes are being taken into account during wage negotiations, then it is not merely those which have just taken place but also those which are bound to occur during the forthcoming year which are going to affect the size of wage claims. If the public utterances of union leaders are anything to go by then the assertion that tax changes are being paid much closer attention during the negotiations of wage settlements at the present time as compared to the 1960s is almost certainly warranted, although in making the above statement one inevitably runs the risk of being accused of casual empiricism. Unfortunately this matter is of considerable importance because if one believes that money-wage claims will be varied in response to either past or expected tax changes then, if the authorities are known to favour higher taxes as a cure for inflation, these actual or expected taxes will themselves turn out to be inflationary via their impact upon money-wage claims. It may well be, therefore, that lower rather than higher taxes are needed in the current crisis, and this is a matter to which we must return in the subsequent chapters on policy.

7 International Aspects of Inflation

It is only during the present decade that proper consideration has been given to the impact of externally generated forces upon an individual country's domestic rate of inflation. There are two reasons in particular why this received comparatively little attention in previous decades. In the first place *The General Theory* was concerned primarily with an assessment of the impact of demand management in a 'closed' economy, that is in an economy whose dependence upon international trade to satisfy domestic demand is very small. That this was so should come as no great surprise in the light of the massive downturn in trade between countries during the inter-war depression. One legacy of *The General Theory* was, however, to distract attention away from the international sector even in the boom years after the war. In the second place it was the United States which played the dominant role in international affairs post-war, and the United States has always been a closed economy by international standards, as is shown by Table 7.1. On the other hand both the United Kingdom and most of the other highly industrialised nations have fairly open economies, and it has been suggested in recent years that the current inflation can be attributed in part to certain changes in the relationship between these countries and the United States which took place during the 1960s.

The question which we seek to answer in this chapter concerns the extent to which a country can import inflation, where imported inflation can be defined as any external influence upon domestic costs and prices. There are, in principle, numerous channels through which inflation generated in one country can be transmitted to another, although they are not necessarily all equally applicable to any one economy at any single time. In reviewing these channels, therefore, it should be borne in mind that we are interested primarily in the extent to which any or all of them can help to account for the accelerated rate of inflation suffered by the United Kingdom since the mid-1960s.

It is useful to begin this section with some figures on the relative openness of different economies. These are set out in Table 7.1.

TABLE 7.1 *Average of exports and imports (of goods and services) as percentage of G.N.P. at current prices in eighteen O.E.C.D. countries*

	1960–2	1968–70	Change
Netherlands	50·2	49·2	−1·0
Belgium	35·5	43·9	+8·4
Norway	40·0	42·6	+2·6
Ireland	38·5	40·6	+2·1
Switzerland	28·3	34·9	+6·6
Denmark	31·9	30·2	−1·7
Austria	24·3	28·2	+3·9
Finland	24·4	26·8	+2·4
Canada	21·2	25·3	+4·1
Sweden	24·3	25·1	+0·8
United Kingdom	22·3	23·5	+1·2
West Germany	18·8	21·9	+3·1
Italy	15·6	19·0	+3·4
Australia	15·4	15·9	+0·5
France	12·8	15·6	+2·8
Spain	10·9	15·3	+4·4
Japan	10·6	10·7	+0·1
United States	4·9	5·9	+1·0

SOURCE: O.E.C.D., *Economic Outlook* (July 1973) p. 84.

Although Table 7.1 does not provide an exact guide to the openness of the economies concerned,[1] it does highlight two important facts, first that the U.S. economy is much less open than those economies with which it conducts most of its trade, and secondly that the United Kingdom is fairly susceptible to internationally generated forces, although much less so than other, smaller economies.

Price Effects

(i) The most obvious impact of external forces upon the United Kingdom's domestic price level is through changes in the prices of non-competitive imports. There are many commodities which cannot be produced within the United Kingdom in any volume, if at all, at the current time. Significant examples are cotton, metals such as zinc, gold and silver, and, in particular, crude oil. In the short term there is virtually nothing which the government can do to curtail demand for these commodities, and even in the long term demand remains relatively inelastic even in the face of substantial price increases. The past decade has seen some of these commodities escalate in price at a staggering rate, the quadrupling of the price of crude oil in the course of one year being a good case in point. It was inevitable, therefore, that the Retail Price Index should be affected, either directly through increases in imported consumer-good prices, or indirectly through increases in manufacturing costs which later showed up in price rises at retail level.

(ii) The situation is, however, rather different if we turn to consider trade in competitive imports, which are primarily manufactured goods. In this context there now exist a number of variants of a model which have in common the distinction between 'competitive' sectors, consisting, *inter alia*, of engineering, chemical and similar industries which must keep their prices in line with those set internationally, and 'sheltered' sectors, consisting largely of nationalised industries and service sectors which are subject to purely domestic pressures.

One variant of the model has been developed with specific reference to the Nordic economies which are highly open. In this model productivity grows faster in competitive sectors than in sheltered sectors. Wages in competitive sectors rise in line with productivity, with profit margins remaining fairly constant. These wage rises then spill over into the sheltered sectors because of union pressure to maintain differentials, with the result that wages in sheltered sectors rise faster than productivity there, and prices are forced upwards by way of compensation to avoid undue erosion of profits. Over all, therefore, domestic prices rise faster than prices in the competitive sector. For this reason it is argued that any changes which do occur in prices set in the competitive sector, which are determined by international forces, will dictate the rate of domestic inflation.

This model is, however, of much less relevance to countries which have smaller competitive sectors, since in these cases neither productivity gains nor wage rises are necessarily greater in such sectors. An alternative model with specific reference to the United Kingdom has been proposed by Congdon.[2] He argues that there was a world-wide investment boom during the latter half of the 1960s. This created a big expansion of demand from overseas for U.K. engineering and electrical goods, and capital goods' prices outpaced those of consumer goods, an unparalleled occurrence in recent economic history. This led to big increases in minimum rates of pay for workers in car plants, engineering workshops, and chemical plants. The boom in demand for capital goods was associated particularly with the 1967 devaluation which cheapened U.K. exports relative to similar products made overseas. Hence Congdon's general conclusion is that 'Inflation emanated from the export sector and was caused by the structural changes necessitated by devaluation.'[3]

The above two sections clearly demonstrate that U.K. domestic prices cannot be isolated from those ruling in other parts of the world. What is not altogether clear from the above, however, is the extent to which the current U.K. inflation is of domestic as opposed to international origin. It is not possible in practice to resolve this issue at all precisely, although a tentative general conclusion is possible. The O.E.C.D., taking the period 1955–70, estimate that[4]

> in the United States, the domestic price influence is massively predominant over competitors' export price influence;
> in Germany and the United Kingdom the domestic price influence is also dominant, but less strongly so;
> in Canada, France and Japan, the influences appear to be more equally weighted;
> in the smaller countries, such as Austria, the Netherlands, Norway and Sweden, the external price influences are considerably more powerful than the domestic influences.

They go on to argue that the above trends are 'in a rough way illustrated by recent parity change behaviour, in as much as the large countries have been forced to make relatively larger parity changes because their trade prices were not kept in line with world market trends on a year to year basis; in the same way the parity changes of large countries may have been less offset by consequential trade price adjustments than in the case of smaller countries'.[5]

It is possible to play down the impact of rising import prices on the basis of the figures given in Table 7.2. The large rise in import prices in late 1967 and early 1969 was due to the 1967 devaluation. Over the four-year period 1966–70 import prices rose by 20·2 per cent, an annual rate of approximately 5 per cent. Given a propensity to import of approximately 20 per cent the average impact of rising import prices upon the Retail Price Index works out at approximately 1 per cent per annum, which is hardly significant relative to the over-all rate of inflation at the time. It should, however, be noted that the commodity boom in the early 1970s, and especially the quadrupling of oil prices, has had a more substantial impact upon retail prices of late.

TABLE 7.2 *Movements in costs and prices (per cent p.a. rate of change)*

	Trend *1959–66*	*1966–7*	*1967–8*	*1968–9*	*1969–70*
Retail prices	3·2	2·5	4·7	5·4	6·9
Consumer prices	3·1	2·5	4·5	5·3	5·3
Hourly wage rates	5·0	4·1	6·8	5·4	10·2
Wages/salaries *per capita*	5·4	5·4	7·7	7·8	12·6
Output *per capita*	2·3	2·3	4·6	2·4	2·1
Import prices	1·3	1·3	11·5	2·6	4·8
Indirect taxes	5·3	−0·1	11·0	14·7	2·5

SOURCE: *National Institute Economic Review* (Feb 1971) p. 38.

International Monetary Effects

In the light of the above it is clear that in so far as the take-off in world-wide rates of inflation during the late 1960s can be attributed to international forces these must have operated primarily through channels other than directly through the prices of imported goods themselves. The principal support for this latter proposition appears essentially as an extension of the Monetarist position, and has been aptly summarised by Johnson in his assertion that 'the rate of inflation in the world economy will be determined by the rate of world monetary expansion relative to the world rate of economic growth'.[6]

A full exposition of this hypothesis has recently been put forward by Duck, Parkin, Rose and Zis.[7] They argue that an important keystone of the international transmission of inflation was the Bretton Woods agreement in 1945 whereby major trading nations agreed to maintain fixed exchange rates except in circumstances of 'fundamental disequilibrium', that is, except where a country was running balance-of-payments deficits year after year because of a long-term deterioration in its ability to compete in international markets. Under the fixed exchange-rate regime, which lasted until 1971, a country which expanded its domestic rate of demand by virtue of an increase in its money supply, necessarily absorbed not only a greater volume of domestic production but also more imported goods as determined by its propensity to import. In so far that a part of this excess demand spilled over into the balance of payments it meant that the inflationary pressure thus generated was divided between the domestic sector and abroad. As a result domestic inflationary pressures were moderated while at the same time inflationary pressure was put upon the rest of the world. The extent of this pressure depended upon the size of the country expanding its money supply relative to the rest of the world. The bigger the country the greater the inflationary pressure created abroad via an excessive rate of its monetary expansion.

Now as Duck *et al.* point out[8]

> Irrevocable fixity of exchange rates with full convertibility of currencies, free trade and unrestricted capital and labour movements link countries together in a world economy in much the same way as regions are linked together in a national economy. In such a world, the general price level and its rate of change would be determined by world aggregate monetary conditions and individual country's price levels and inflation rates would stay in line with the world average and with each other.

Let us consider by way of illustration what will happen in a fixed exchange-rate regime where a large country increases its money supply starting from a position of full employment. Assuming that this country begins in a situation of balance-of-payments equilibrium the resultant excess demand will create a balance-of-payments deficit which must be counterbalanced by surpluses elsewhere in the world. These surpluses will tend in turn to create inflationary pressures in three respects. First, the expansion of their export sectors will create excess demand in surplus countries unless they begin in a situation of considerable under-employment. Secondly, expectations of the future rate of inflation will be revised upwards in surplus countries, either because of the direct pressure upon the price level exerted by the newly created excess demand, or because of demonstration effects created by observation of accelerating inflation in the deficit country. Thirdly, the money supply of the surplus countries will be growing more rapidly than it would otherwise because of additions to their reserves,[9] just as the growth in the money supply of the deficit country will be slowed down by the loss of reserves. However, if this situation were to be allowed to continue for long enough, both deficits and surpluses might become unmanageably large. Each country is therefore obliged in a fixed exchange-rate regime to introduce controls over domestic demand in order to eliminate its payments imbalance. In practice this can only be achieved in the long term by *keeping all countries' rates of inflation at a similar level.*

Now in applying the above line of argument to the post-war world two obvious facts need to be established if the argument is to be considered sound. In the first place it must be shown that exchange rates were indeed fixed with few exceptions, since exchange-rate flexibility, for reasons set out below, would enable an individual country to insulate itself to some extent from externally generated inflation, and hence would permit it to hold its rate of inflation below the level prevailing elsewhere in the world. Secondly, it must be demonstrated that excessive monetary expansion in a large country created world excess demand and hence caused the world rate of inflation to rise sharply during the late 1960s and early 1970s.

Between 1956 and 1970 there were only six changes in exchange rates[10] among the ten major world currencies. In the light of the strains imposed during this period upon several of these currencies, and especially upon sterling, this was a good record for the system, especially in view of the increased liberalisation of trade and capital movements during this period.[11] It is therefore reasonable to categorise this period as one of exchange-rate fixity.

The monetary stimulus, it is argued, came from the United States. Duck *et al.*[12] contend that 'the world inflation of the late 1960's was the outcome of excessive nominal demand expansion in the U.S.A. which spread via the flows of money and demand associated with the deterioration of the U.S. trade position to the rest of the Dollar Standard world'. Similarly, Laidler, using the inflation rate in the United States as a proxy for the world rate has concluded that

> Systematic though variations in the British inflation rate may have been, it has fluctuated around quite different average levels at different times. These average levels have not deviated far from the long-run world inflation rate, represented by the United States-rate. . . . Only since 1949 has the British inflation rate been systematically above the U.S. rate, but it has taken two devaluations to permit this. Just as, incidentally, Germany's very low rate of inflation has had to be accompanied by an upward drift in the value of the mark.[13]

That the monetary stimulus should have originated in the United States is by no means surprising. The U.S. economy has always been a closed economy, which meant that its domestic policy was not seriously constrained by anxieties about the effects of monetary expansion upon the balance of payments, at least until the very end of the period under consideration. Those who support the idea of the United States exporting inflation via substantial balance-of-payment deficits argue that these arose principally as a direct consequence of the war in Vietnam[14] which the U.S. government was unwilling to pay for via increased taxation, although it is sometimes suggested that the Vietnam war served only to exacerbate an underlying trend in rising prices which would anyway have served to accelerate the rate of world inflation during the late 1960s. In other words, it is alleged that since the only alternative to higher taxation facing the U.S. government was to increase the money supply, they chose to follow this course of action, and in so doing they created excess domestic demand which in turn led to substantial balance-of-payments deficits.

There appears, however, to be only limited evidence of the United States exporting inflation prior to 1969. On the one hand, Duck *et al.* argue that 'world inflation accelerated in the late 1960s because of the emergence at that time of overall world excess demand for both goods and labour',[15] and Nordhaus also concludes that 'The wage inflation in the United States and Canada can be attributed to the tightness of the labour markets. Outside of North America the rise in wages can be more tenably ascribed to the permissive economic climate generated by a rise in import prices.'[16] On the other hand, there are discernible trends in major variables which indicate the need for caution.

In the first place, between 1948 and 1967 the United States shared with West Germany the distinction of having the lowest annual rate of price increase (1·7 per cent p.a.) of the ten major industrial countries of the world.[17] In the second place, between 1948 and 1967 the United States had the lowest rate of monetary expansion of any of the ten countries (2·4 per cent p.a.).[1] 'Although the rate of expansion did begin to accelerate after 1965, it rose at an even faster rate in virtually all of the other countries under consideration.[19] And in the third place, the U.S. balance of payments appears to have had only minor repercussions on the rest of the world prior to 1970. The O.E.C.D., for example, have estimated that of the number of cases in which other O.E.C.D. countries' surpluses on non-monetary transactions is taken as a rough indication of the extent to which the U.S. deficits had significant monetary repercussions on the surplus countries, then it was not until 1971 that a significant impact is discernible.[20] From 1965 to 1967 the over-all U.S. deficit was quite small in relation to the expansion of the money supply in other O.E.C.D. countries. In 1968 and 1969 the U.S. balance of payments was in surplus on an official settlements basis,[21] and thus had a contractionary effect upon the total money supply of other O.E.C.D. countries. In 1970 the U.S. balance of payments went heavily into deficit, flooding other countries with money via increased reserves, although it would appear that a significant proportion of this money was neutralised by the central banks of recipient countries via, for example, open-market operations. It was only in 1971 that a further massive deficit in the U.S. balance of payments went hand in hand with a greatly accelerated growth in the money supply of other O.E.C.D. countries.

Some idea of the sums involved can be obtained by reference to Table 7.3. Given that the years 1971 and 1972 correspond with the period when prices either remained at an historically high level, or continued to accelerate in most O.E.C.D. countries, it is evident that the international monetarist theory of inflation has a much more plausible ring about it with respect to this period than it does with respect to the period 1965–9. That the U.K. wage explosion was closely linked to internationally generated forces during the early 1970s is supported by Duck *et al.*,[22] Nordhaus[23] and Goldstein,[24] who argues that 'The pattern of reserve accruals by non-U.S. central banks lends support to the theory of exported inflation (or perhaps more accurately of imported money supply increases) for the 1970–72 biennium.'

TABLE 7.3 *Changes in international reserves in some leading industrial countries*

	1967–8 $ m.	1969–70 $ m.	1971–3 $ m.
Belgium	−163	+660	+1023
Canada	+342	+1663	+1371
France	−2532	+759	+5055
West Germany	+1919	+3662	+10175
Italy	+429	+11	+727
Japan	+887	+1934	+13525
Netherlands	+81	+771	+1551
Switzerland	+748	+839	+2356
United Kingdom	−677	+405	+2820

SOURCE: Goldstein, *National Westminster Bank Review* (Nov 1974) p. 21.

Goldstein blames the deterioration in the U.S. balance of payments during 1971 and 1972 upon 'the exceptionally rapid increase in real G.N.P. during 1972, a higher price for oil imports, the growing ability of less-developed countries to supply a wide range of manufactures to the U.S. market, and the sluggishness of its producers in adjusting product-lines to meet changing competitive conditions'.[25] He also goes on to note the discrepancy between the U.S. balance on current account, constituting deficits of $3817 million in 1971 and $9807 million in 1972 respectively, and official reserve transactions, constituting deficits of $30,470 million in 1971 and $11,064 million in 1972 respectively.[26] The difference between these magnitudes largely constitutes massive speculative capital outflows which, in this particular case, were moving out of dollars and into relatively undervalued currencies such as the mark and the yen, as shown in Table 7.3 above. These figures, incidentally, exclude the $60,000 million or so of Eurodollar holdings which were floating around Europe at the time.[27]

Despite the apparent strength of the above argument it nevertheless lacks universal appeal. The O.E.C.D. contend, for example, that in view of the easing of demand pressures in many countries during 1971 and 1972 acceptance of what they call the 'international-liquidity-monetarist' explanation of the course of inflation in O.E.C.D. countries other than the United States 'required the assumption that an abnormally high rate of money creation has a direct impact on price and wage determination, independent of any effect on spending decisions and real demand'.[28] However, they have little faith in this eventuality, and their over-all conclusion is that the international-liquidity-monetarist explanation of inflation is highly unsatisfactory taking the period 1965–72 as a whole.

It is clear from the above discussion that the international-monetarist hypothesis exhibits many of the characteristics which prove so frustrating to those who seek to analyse the current inflation. We have noted in particular that data generated from a common source, in this case the O.E.C.D., can seemingly be interpreted in such a way as to demonstrate either that imported money-supply increases have long been an important determinant of the current inflation,[29] or that this factor can largely be discounted.[30] However, one possible conclusion which does require further consideration from the viewpoint of current policy measures is that which states that under a fixed exchange-rate regime an individual country's rate of inflation must fall into line with rates prevailing elsewhere in the world. In this context we must conclude this chapter by asking what effects may result from the change-over from a fixed exchange rate regime to a regime of floating exchange rates.

Since 1971 the major currencies of the world have been floating in relation to one another, although the extent of the ('managed') float has been kept within bounds considered to be desirable by individual countries. Now we have already noted that a country which suffers from excess domestic demand can, under a fixed exchange-rate regime, export a part of its inflation via spillover effects into imports. The introduction of a floating exchange-rate regime, however, helps to protect a country from imported inflation. This is essentially because under a fixed exchange-rate regime, if a country is initially suffering from excess domestic demand which is forcing up its prices relative to those abroad, the purchase of imports becomes an increasingly attractive proposition. But if its exchange rate is allowed simultaneously to depreciate then relative prices remain unaffected. Hence the spillover effect is greatly reduced and rather less of the domestically generated inflation will find its way overseas. In so far as floating exchange rates also necessarily imply that individual countries amass neither substantial balance-of-payments deficits nor surpluses, such rates make it possible for a country to protect its internal monetary system against an uncontrollably large influx of reserves.

The introduction of floating exchange rates therefore serves to bottle up inflationary pressures within their country of origin. That this is so has important implications from a policy point of view. Under the fixed exchange-rate regime monetary measures introduced in order to control domestic inflation could be frustrated by the leakages which affect an open economy. There was, for example, little point in a country contracting its domestically generated money supply when this was accompanied by an influx of reserves which resulted from the reduction in imports and transference of production to the export sector. However, under a floating exchange-rate regime contraction of the money supply can be accompanied by an appreciation of the currency which serves to forestall the adverse impact of a potentially large balance-of-payments surplus.

It can, however, be argued that floating exchange rates not merely widen differentials between rates of inflation in different countries but also serve to raise the average rate of inflation suffered by countries as a whole. Two arguments in particular are proposed to support this contention. In the first place it is argued that, whereas under a fixed exchange-rate regime an individual country's excess demand is dissipated over a wide area where it can be dealt with fairly easily, under a floating exchange-rate regime it is bottled up in the country of origin where it can be offset only through the introduction of undesirably stringent contractionary measures. In the second place it is contended that democratic governments are naturally prone to pursue expansionary policies. Under a fixed exchange-rate regime such tendencies are suppressed by a strong distaste for the devaluation which is almost certain to be an eventual necessity in the absence of government self control, whereas under a floating exchange-rate regime expansion can take place without inhibition.

It would appear on balance, however, that the introduction of managed floating in 1971–2 has had a beneficial impact. As Goldstein points out[31]

> Much of the recent world inflation would probably never have occurred if the other major currencies had been floating against

the U.S. dollar. For then the massive U.S. payments deficits of 1971 and 1972 would never have developed. In the absence of those deficits the expansion of the domestic money supply in a number of leading industrial countries would presumably have been markedly reduced, along with the subsequent pressure of excess demand.

Certainly the reduction of non-U.S. reserve accruals which followed upon the transition to managed floating went hand in hand with a successful attempt to curb money-supply growth in leading industrial countries.[32] Whether or not one expects as a consequence a lagged downwards adjustment of the rate of inflation in the countries concerned depends, of course, upon the extent of one's belief in the international-monetarist hypothesis. Whatever one's views on this question it seems hard to deny, however, that the proponents of the international-monetarist hypothesis, which encompasses matters considered both in this and the two preceding chapters, have the best-developed explanation of the current inflation, even if future events should happen to prove it incorrect.

8 The Role of the Trade Unions

A Brief History of Wage Bargaining

One very contentious aspect of the current inflation unquestionably concerns the role played by the trade unions. This is a topic which elicits the expression of extreme viewpoints from economists and general public alike, although not necessarily for the same reasons. That this is so is far from surprising since it is manifestly true that unions do play an active role in the generation of inflation, in that it is they who actually demand higher wages. What is at issue, however, is whether the role played by the unions actually *causes* inflation. On the one hand, there is a school of thought which blames the unions more or less exclusively for the increased pace of inflation. On the other hand, there are several schools of thought, amongst them the Monetarists, who absolve the unions from virtually all blame, largely on the premise that apparently inflationary wage demands are, in reality, attempts by the unions to maintain the standard of living of their members which has been steadily eroded by forces outside their control.

Now we have already noted that there was a marked deterioration in the inflation–unemployment trade-off during the late 1960s. Clearly, therefore, if the unions were to blame for this deterioration then there must have been some marked changes taking place within the unions themselves at the time. In order to clarify what these might have been it is appropriate to explore, albeit briefly, the history of collective bargaining in the United Kingdom.[1]

In the early days of unionisation wages were determined largely by the forces of competition in product markets. Wage bargaining took place on an establishment basis, and firms could not afford to grant wage rises greater than those being conceded elsewhere, since they would subsequently have been unable to raise their prices by way of compensation without loss of custom. Hence the understanding developed that wage rises would need to be small and infrequent, and would depend primarily upon the state of the trade cycle.

During the First World War collective bargaining took place increasingly on an industry-wide basis. Now this meant (1) that employers could potentially afford to let wages rise rather more frequently than had been the custom in the past, since all firms within an industry would need to raise their prices by an equivalent amount in order to protect their profits, and (2) that unions could potentially use the threat of strike action to greater effect since the entire industry, rather than individual firms, would be affected were a work stoppage to take place. However, the 1920s and 1930s proved to be years of widespread economic depression with the result that the unions were unable for the most part to put their new-found strength to the test.

The Second World War, however, heralded in a new era in collective bargaining. Successive governments committed themselves to the maintenance of full employment even at the cost of continued inflation. Unions soon discovered that higher wages no longer resulted in higher unemployment, and hence began to look around for a new standard on which to base wage demands. For the most part they settled upon two main principles; first that wages should go up every year without fail, and secondly that wages should rise by an amount determined by pay awards to 'equivalent' workers in other industries. In addition, however, some unions began to question the whole concept of historically determined differentials and set out to elevate themselves in the wages 'league table'. It is often pointed out that this process has gone hand in hand with the transference of power from the union hierarchy to shop stewards in close contact with the shop floor. It is argued further that shop stewards are, as a group, more militant than either the union hierarchy or the rank and file. Whether this has changed the attitudes of unions to wage bargaining is itself a matter of some debate since the job of a union negotiator, at whatever the level, is to convey the wishes of the rank and file rather than his own personal feelings to the management. Whatever the reason, however, it is argued that the unions have become increasingly militant in their approach to collective bargaining and that this has manifested itself in the heightened incidence of strike activity which we noted in Table 1.2 (p. 4).

Now, irrespective of where the impetus towards increased militancy originated, there can be no doubt that the early 1960s provided a favourable environment for increased union pressure in the wages field. First of all most firms were able, by raising their prices, to pass on to their customers the impact of higher wages. Secondly, even if higher wages did result in some redundancies, it was relatively easy for redundant workers to find alternative employment. Thirdly, improved benefits for the unemployed provided a cushion for redundant workers who could not immediately find alternative work. Fourthly, from the employer's point of view the cost of facing out a strike was more often than not a good deal more expensive in the short term than an increased wage bill. Finally, the structure of the economy was such that certain groups of workers, for example the dockers, could, by withdrawing their labour, severely curtail output and employment throughout the entire economy.

The Sociological Theory of Inflation

But what is particularly significant is that the unemployment–inflation trade-off did not deteriorate markedly until the *late* 1960s, by which time the factors described above had been in force for a good many years. So how can the blame for this deterioration be placed at the door of the trade unions? The answer is contained in what is currently referred to as the 'sociological' or 'institutional' theory of inflation. This theory argues that the problem of inflation can no longer be tackled by reference either to any of the economic theories previously expounded or to such aspects of the collective bargaining situation as disturbed differentials. According to Phelps-Brown[2] the problem is that

> collective bargaining today is not between labour and capital, or employees and management, for the distribution of the products of particular industries between pay and profit; but between

> different groups of employees, for the distribution of the national product between them one with another, and between them as a whole and the inactive population. Cost inflation appears basically as the process by which particular groups of employees enter and enforce claims to shares in the national product that add up to more than the total product.

The chief advocate of the sociological theory is Wiles.[3] As he sees it trade-union jealousy is the motive force behind the current inflation. He envisages inflation depending upon 'what numbers trade union leaders pick out of the air when they make wage claims. For the claims are entirely subjective.'[4] In the making of these claims little account is taken of any unemployment which may result since 'social services and tax rebates will cushion those laid off well enough for the period extending to the trade-union leader's time horizon'.[5] Furthermore, although many wage claims may appear absurdly high, this kind of behaviour should be seen simply as a reflection of the deterioration in the national character. Thus 'in a nation where the national character is plainly changing – rising crime, sex-and-drug permissiveness, less self-discipline in dress, speech and deportment, less respect for hard work, less religion, loosening of the nuclear family, breakdown of a deferential class structure, etc., etc. – we must also expect less restraint at the bargaining table, less concern for consequences'.[6]

Thus the nub of the sociological theory is that inflation results from trade unions trampling over all and sundry who stand in their way, in an attempt to obtain a bigger share of the national cake for their members. They know their own strength and they are prepared to use it irrespective of whether either society as a whole or their fellow trade unionists suffer as a result. This procedure is, however, largely self-defeating because each union is determined to maintain its wage differentials *vis-à-vis* all others, and each excessive pay award is followed by many others of like size. Thus at the end of the day inflation has escalated out of all proportion but almost no one is satisfied.

Now the above propositions are all very well but as they stand they contain rather more conjecture than demonstrable fact. In order, therefore, to establish more clearly the role played by the unions we must begin by setting down some testable hypotheses. These are conveniently provided by Mulvey and Trevithick as follows.[7]

(*a*) Trade unions 'rubber stamp' wage adjustments determined by market forces;

(*b*) By exercising their market power trade unions are able to produce an inflationary bias in the labour market such that the rate of inflation will always be greater by a constant amount than that which would have existed had the unions not exercised that power;

(*c*) Trade unions are able to accelerate the rate of inflation when aggregate demand is at a low level, but as excess demand develops strongly a point will be reached at which union activity, because of its bureaucratic nature, and its need to operate through the periodic and time-consuming process of collective bargaining, will secure rather lower wage increases than the free market would have permitted; and

(*d*) Bureaucratic unions, adopting collective-bargaining processes, will always secure lower wage settlements than a free labour market would permit.

Now it is customary to assume that the organisation of workers into unions will make their collective bargaining power greater than the sum of the bargaining power of each individual. The advantages most often cited are:

(1) The union can afford professional management and advice when preparing wage claims – it can also afford to collect relevant information about the company and the economy generally to support its claim;

(2) It can threaten a strike by most or all of its members if it does not get its way; and

(3) It can plan its strategies in the light of the over-all aims of the union movement, which are political as well as economic.

From the unions' point of view the information most worthwhile to collect for bargaining purposes is that on prices, profitability and productivity. But in so far as it takes some time to prepare a carefully argued case for a wage rise there are likely to be delays in the reaction of unions to changes in market circumstances. In this respect it is important to distinguish the argument that the unions will obtain a wage rise as large as market forces permit once a short interval of time has passed, from the argument that the time and trouble of preparing for collective bargaining will not permit trade unions to obtain as much money as their members could have done while acting on an individual basis, were the latter to react immediately to favourable market conditions. Superficially, at least, the latter argument is the less plausible of the two.

Now if the unions are using their strength to good effect in driving up their wages this should show up by way of an improvement in the rewards to unionised workers relative to those gained by their non-unionised counterparts. But although we might intuitively expect wage differentials between the unionised and non-unionised sectors to widen continually, there are some grounds in practice for not expecting this to occur. In the first place, employers of non-unionised workers who wish to prevent them from organising may have to pay them a wage sufficiently high as to remove that temptation. In the second place, pay awards to non-unionised workers which go to arbitration may well be judged largely on the basis of wages earned by comparable unionised workers. Hence improved union pay scales are often associated in practice with improvements of like amount for non-unionised workers.

In the light of the above it is appropriate to argue that trade unions may be regarded as an independent cause of inflation if it can be demonstrated that they have exercised their market power in such a way as, either to widen the wage differential between unionised and non-unionised sectors of the work-force, or to increase the proportion of the work-force paid higher union rates.

Militancy

But a major difficulty now arises in that if the trade unions are to be blamed for causing inflation it must be conclusively demonstrated that any changes in wages and prices which have occurred are the direct consequences of the exercise of trade-union power. In other words, the trade unions must be shown to be acting quite independently of changes in aggregate demand. In order to resolve this difficulty it is necessary to have recourse to the concept of union *militancy* since we seek to establish a direct link between union aggressiveness and the rate of inflation. But union militancy is not a quantifiable variable as such, so that we must use a proxy variable in order to measure the degree of militancy. Over the years a wide selection of proxies have been used to test the relationship between militancy and inflation, so it is appropriate to give detailed consideration to some of these below.

In assessing these proxy variables it should be borne in mind that they should satisfy a number of different criteria.[8] First, they should be based upon objective data; secondly, they should respond to subtle changes in pressure exerted by unions; thirdly, they should unambiguously measure union militancy and not be subject to alternative interpretations such as that they measure employer resistance; finally, and most importantly, they should be related to 'a reasonably well-formed theory of wage determination'.

(i) Subjective estimates

An early attempt to derive a subjective index of union militancy based upon a five-point rating was made by Dicks-Mireaux and Dow.[9] Measures of this kind, however, clearly fail to meet the objectivity criterion and there is no interest currently being expressed in this approach.

(ii) Industrial profitability

During the early 1960s considerable interest was expressed in measuring the relationship between wage-rate changes and industrial profitability. However, although some evidence was forthcoming at the time to suggest that union militancy tended to increase at times of high industrial profitability,[10] the experience of the early 1970s has lent no support to this hypothesis since wage rates and profits have, for the most part, moved inversely rather than in conjunction.

(iii) The proportion of the labour force organised in unions/The rate of change of the proportion of the labour force organised in unions

Hines has argued in studies spanning a decade[11] that the rate of change of money wages is determined by (*a*) the level of unionisation existing in any time period and (*b*) the rate of change of unionisation in that period. His basic line of argument is that rising union membership both before and during wage negotiations makes union leaders more militant, producing similar attitudes on the shop floor. For their part, employers come increasingly to fear the threat of strike action and the costs associated with it, with the result that they grow increasingly willing to concede wage claims. This hypothesis has, however, been widely criticised.[12] Purdy and Zis, in particular, argue that Hines's case is both theoretically and empirically weak. They criticise Hines's unionisation statistics and suggest that if they are improved then the acceleration in wage rates during the late 1960s can no longer be explained by reference to Hines's militancy variables. In their opinion 'a retesting of Hines' complete wage determination equation on the basis of improved data and consistent definitions of variables is considerably less than Hines claims, and also that the level of unemployment cannot be ignored in comparisons of wage movements between the inter-war and post-war periods'.

Purdy and Zis argue further that the rate of change of unionisation is a poor proxy measure of union militancy.[13]

> Each pay claim submitted by a union can potentially lead to a strike and hence to a (temporary) loss of earnings by the workers involved. By joining the appropriate union immediately before and during pay negotiations workers may minimise their financial loss by securing entitlement to strike benefit in the event that negotiations actually do break down. During pay negotiations, therefore, an increase in the rate of change of unionisation over and above that which would otherwise be forthcoming would occur, not as a result of active union recruitment but of the actions of marginal union members who wished to increase their personal security. The aggregate rate of change of unionisation would on this hypothesis depend on the proportion of workers with pay claims pending during any given period and on the probability with which marginal union members in any given bargaining unit expected their negotiations to terminate in a strike.

(iv) Strike activity

Considerable support for the use of data on strike activity as a proxy for union militancy is to be found in the work of Godfrey and Taylor.[14] In their joint study the authors found that changes in the number of stoppages at work due to industrial disputes had a significant influence upon the rate of wage inflation. In individual studies

Godfrey found that the number of stoppages in all industries other than mining was closely correlated with the rate of change of money wages, and Taylor found, among other things, that of the 8 per cent rise in earnings between 1969 and 1970, strikes, as measured by the number of working days lost, were responsible for approximately 4 per cent.

However the use of data on strike activity as a proxy for union militancy has been widely criticised.[15] Bean and Peel argue that it is invalid to hypothesise union militancy as a cause of inflation on the basis of data on all strikes irrespective of cause. They contend[16] that 'Strikes relating to the category "claims for wage increases" accounted in 1962 for only 28% of the total number of strikes for all industries except mining',[17] and 'for 57% of the total' in 1970. They then go on to discuss whether strike activity should be measured by (*a*) the number of stoppages, (*b*) the number of workers involved, or (*c*) the number of working days lost. This is an important matter because as is shown by Table 1.2 (p. 4) these three variables do not always move in the same direction. Bean and Paul themselves reject data on working days lost (the index used by Taylor) on the grounds that 'Any given number of working days lost, for instance, could be the result of a one-day stoppage in an entire industry, or the result of a protracted dispute in only a single company.'

Bean and Peel, like Taylor and Godfrey, favour the index of the number of stoppages. Purdy and Zis argue, however, that the official statistics ignore 'many forms of industrial action short of striking ranging from go-slows and bans on overtime working to less palpable actions such as the withdrawal of co-operation from management . . . as well as a large number of short, small-scale work stoppages'.[18] Hence they are led on to ask whether 'a large number of short and small-scale strikes indicate more or less militancy than a smaller number of longer and larger scale strikes?'[19] They also argue that 'an increase in strike activity in a sector in which the strike is already a normal occurrence' should be regarded as less significant from the point of view of measuring union militancy than 'an increase in a sector where strikes are relatively rare'.

It should be noted that Godfrey and Taylor in their individual studies use strike-frequency figures on a quarterly and semi-annual basis respectively. But both strikes and earnings changes have a strong seasonal element[20] so that the correlation between these variables may be biased upwards as a result. It is also of considerable interest that over the past few years the great bulk of strike activity has originated in the public sector. During the 1960s the public-sector industries bore the brunt of the various prices-and-incomes policies then in force, and earnings lagged behind those in the private sector. It is therefore perfectly plausible to argue that the current wave of strikes within the public sector is not so much an attempt to force up the level of wage rates generally as an attempt to restore differentials between public and private sectors which had been eroded during the 1960s. From this, one can derive the hypothesis that far from strike activity leading to inflation, inflation is the prime cause of strike activity.[21]

Grossman[22] argues that the recent high incidence of strike activity is a manifestation of rapidly changing inflationary expectations. Thus when 'expectations are in a ferment, they are also likely to become more dispersed. Opinions tend to differ more frequently and also to be held with less certainty. Consequently, greater differences arise between union and management assessments of what employers can afford to pay, with both sides playing for a margin of safety.'

Certainly there are good grounds for bringing employers' attitudes into consideration. It clearly takes two sides to make a fight. Hence, as Purdy and Zis point out, 'strike frequency may just as well be taken as an index of employers' resistance'.[23] In view of this they see any further discussion about the measurement of union militancy as 'a futile exercise without the construction of a more rigorous model of union–employer negotiations'. Their general conclusion is therefore one of 'extreme scepticism towards any policy recommendations based on the existing studies of union militancy and wage inflation'.[24] This conclusion is also found by Ward and Zis[25] to apply equally well to Belgium, France, Italy, West Germany and the Netherlands.

(v) Spillovers and key bargains

An alternative explanation of the way unions can cause inflation is contained in a wage-leadership model which hypothesises that substantial wage rises obtained by a key group of workers spill over into other sectors of the labour market.[26] In its commonest form this model hypothesises that the key group, which generally contains skilled manual workers, is able to take advantage of persistent excess demand for its services, in order to push up its wages in advance of other sectors of the labour market, whereupon other groups of workers successfully demand whatever wage increases are necessary in order to preserve wage differentials relative to the key group. Unlike key-sector wage increases, however, these latter increases bear little relationship to the state of demand for the workers concerned. Hence wages over all can be seen to rise independently of the state of excess demand.

An alternative explanation of the spillover mechanism argues that wages rise in the fastest-growing industries at a rate more or less in line with the rate of productivity growth. Once again wages rise in other sectors in order to preserve differentials, with the result that wages rise over all much faster than does average productivity.

In order to test these hypotheses it is necessary to specify the key sectors which act as wage leaders. Eckstein and Wilson, for the United States, selected a group of industries in the Mid-West which are highly unionised and highly concentrated. Hines, for the United Kingdom, selected a group of predominantly public-sector industries such as gas, electricity and transport. Mulvey and Trevithick, for the Republic of Ireland, selected a group encompassing electricians, mechanical fitters, motor mechanics, plumbers, bricklayers and sheet-metal workers. In all cases limited support was forthcoming for the wage-leadership model, although it should be borne in mind that none of these studies cover the recent period of rapid wage escalation.

There are, however, a number of problems associated with wage-leadership models. The principal difficulty has to do with the lack of a well-constructed theory of the spillover mechanism. As Mulvey and Trevithick themselves point out,[27] for example, their interpretation of the operation of the wage-determination proces in Ireland is 'partly impressionistic'. There is additionally the customary ambiguity about the econometric results. As Burton points out[28]

> The competitive model of wage determination also predicts that wages will move in like fashion in different sectors of the labour market (given certain assumptions) as a result of inter-sectoral labour supply shifts in response to changes in the relative net advantages of various occupations. What could be useful here are disaggregative labour-market studies to test whether similar wage increases are brought about through the agency of labour

supply shifts (market pressure) or coercive actions (union pressure).

Conclusions

In view of the above difficulties it seems reasonable to concur with the opinion of Purdy and Zis that 'the existing studies of the role of unions in the inflationary process are of little value in helping to reveal either the causes of inflation or the appropriateness and effectiveness of possible remedies'.[29] However, it is inappropriate to infer from the lack of hard-and-fast evidence about the role of unions in the inflationary process that they are, by implication, wholly blameless. Of the four alternatives proposed by Mulvey and Trevithick, to which previous reference has been made (pp. 94–5), the first and last are clearly of little relevance at the present time. But whereas one can accept the proposition that trade-union aggressiveness does contribute periodically to the acceleration of the rate of inflation, one must equally accept that trade-union behaviour is more often than not dependent upon economic forces. Turner was clearly of this opinion in arguing that 'it should by now be very clear, not merely that unions are far from being the only significant factor in the inflationary situation, but that they are not generally an independent factor in it'.[30] Mulvey and Trevithick are of like mind. They conclude that[31] 'trade union activity does, in certain circumstances at least, introduce an inflationary bias into the labour market', although 'the impact of the union may be negligible or even negative'.

As should by now have become abundantly clear there is remarkably little that can be said with any degree of certainty about the causes of the current inflation. Investigations into the extent to which the trade unions have played an independent role in the acceleration of the rate of inflation during the 1970s have been dogged by continued controversy.[32] It is all too easy to point to the outward manifestations of union aggressiveness and to link them directly to the changes in the price level. An overriding need remains for a clear and unambiguous explanation of the precise reason why the late 1960s was such a crucial period with regard to the inflation–unemployment trade-off. To argue, as does one eminent proponent of the sociological view, that 'In country after country the time must have come when the number with solely postwar experience attained a critical mass, sufficient to outweigh the force of tradition and the respect accorded to older men',[33] is far from satisfactory not merely as a statement in its own right but especially when viewed in relation to the stream of empirical evidence disgorged in support of alternative schools of thought. Regrettably, there are no indications that this difficulty will be resolved within the foreseeable future. At the end of the day, therefore, it is difficult to avoid the conclusion that the reader's own prejudices towards the trade-union movement will continue to exercise a dominant role when the time comes either to blame the trade unions, or to absolve them from all blame, for causing inflation.

Part 4
Cures for the Current Inflation

9 Introduction and Résumé

Before embarking upon the task of examining in detail the various weapons in the government's armoury appropriate to the control of inflation, we can usefully pause to remind ourselves at this point of the possible causes of inflation to which we have assigned some significance. This exercise is worthwhile because, as pointed out previously, there is no single remedy which is guaranteed to eliminate inflation irrespective of its origins. In the paragraphs below the appropriate remedies are outlined alongside each causal factor, and we will have these connections in mind when we subsequently consider the government's options in the current crisis.

As should by now be clear there are currently two predominant schools of thought about inflation. On the one hand, we have the school of thought, consisting of a slightly curious mixture of Monetarists and post-Keynesians, who blame inflation upon economic forces, specifically the continued existence of excess demand. On the other hand, we have the school of thought who blame inflation upon sociological and institutional forces. We will consider these schools separately below.

Excess-demand theories

We have referred to these theories under the umbrella title of the expectations-augmented Phillips Curve. Adherents of these theories all believe that the Phillips Curve offers the possibility of a trade-off between inflation and unemployment in the short run, although the possibility of a long-run trade-off is a matter of some dispute. They also believe that the existence of excess demand is a pre-condition for an inflationary spiral, which they argue is fuelled by expectations of future price rises. The Monetarists believe that this excess demand is created via an excess supply of money, which in turn has its origins both in domestic events such as Budget deficits financed by the banking sector, and in international events such as balance-of-payments surpluses. More specifically they point to the large balance-of-payments deficits and capital outflows associated with the United States during the period of the Vietnam war as a major source of internationally transmitted inflation during the late 1960s, and to central and local government profligacy as a continuing major source of domestically created money. In this respect they differ from the post-Keynesians who do not assign any particular importance to the growth in the money supply as such. Rather, post-Keynesians contend that although excess demand does stem primarily from the addiction of governments to overspending, and hence to Budget deficits, they see these as essentially *fiscal* actions. In their opinion the money supply is left free by the authorities to adjust upwards in line with increases in prices which have already taken place.

Monetarists and post-Keynesians are also in part-agreement about how to control inflation. The first item on the Monetarist agenda is to let the exchange rate float freely in order to isolate the U.K. money supply from imported money flows. Secondly, they want the Bank of England to keep a tight rein upon the money supply and upon the rate of domestic credit expansion. In this latter respect they would like the government to avoid excessively large Budget deficits, or, if this is unavoidable in the short term, to finance any such deficits through the sale of government securities to the private sector rather than through the expansion of the money supply. Post-Keynesians in their turn place great store by fiscal actions. Like the Monetarists they too would like to see substantial cuts in public expenditure as well as curbs upon consumer expenditure exercised via the tax system. If this is done, they argue, then there will be no need for any further increases in the money supply.

Both Monetarists and post-Keynesians would also like to see measures introduced with a view to shifting the natural rate of unemployment to the left. Furthermore, the majority of both groups support the idea of widespread indexation of economic variables such as wages, interest rates, profits and dividends. However, the one policy instrument in which they have little or no faith is a prices-and-incomes policy because they do not believe that this has been of any value in the past except perhaps the voluntary policy introduced shortly after the end of the Second World War.

Sociological/Institutional theories

These theories, the latter-day equivalents of the cost-push theories of the 1960s, argue that the current inflation is caused by forces which are unrelated to economic factors such as the state of excess demand. Rather, the causal agent is said to be trade-union monopoly control over the supply of labour in key sectors of the economy. It is argued that powerful trade unions, inspired by jealousy of pay rises obtained by comparable groups either at home or abroad, exercise their power to obtain even larger pay increases for their members. But the struggle to keep ahead of rival groups involves unions in a never-ending rat-race which quickly causes pay claims to escalate as union leaders pluck numbers from the air. Furthermore, given an institutional framework within which the remuneration of different groups of workers is closely interrelated via historically determined differentials, the pay of weak groups is also pulled upwards broadly in line with the gains of the powerful, except in times of heavy unemployment.

The corollary of the above processes is that the Phillips Curve ceases to have any relevance whatsoever for inflation control. Increasing the pool of the unemployed cannot ameliorate the rate of inflation because wage claims are unrelated to the state of excess demand. Hence monetary and fiscal measures are inappropriate forms of control. What is needed is a prices-and-incomes policy which acts directly to hold down the rate of increase of wages and earnings. Alternatively, trade-union power must be curbed via legislation designed to outlaw certain practices, such as picketing involving violence, employed by unions to achieve their ends.

10 Prices-and-Incomes Policy

Prices-and-incomes policies as the cure for inflation are espoused by the sociological school who lay the blame for inflation at the door of the trade unions. During the post-war period the majority of governments in power have seen considerable merit in such policies despite a growing volume of evidence as to their inability to reduce the rate of inflation in anything other than the very short term. Both the current Labour administration and the 'Opposition' appear at long last to have learnt the lessons of history in this respect, although as a matter of political expediency the Labour Party, in particular, continues to cling to prices-and-incomes policies as the 'least undesirable' method of containing inflation. In the course of this chapter we seek to review past policies and to assess their effectiveness. This will then enable us to draw certain conclusions as to the desirability of continuing with such policies in the future.

Past Policies

Various governments have attempted to restrain prices and incomes over the post-war period.[1] Controls were introduced in 1948–50, 1956,[2] 1961 (in the form of a 'pay pause') and 1962–4 (in the form of 'guideposts' for prices and incomes). During 1964 the National Board for Prices and Incomes was established to supersede the

National Incomes Commission and advance warning of wage and price changes was required. In July 1966 prices and incomes were 'frozen' for six months, and this was followed by a further six months of 'severe restraint'. Between 1968 and 1972 there was no official policy as such but wage and price increases were supposedly determined by reference to such criteria as productivity increases. A tripartite policy was in operation from November 1972 until October 1974, followed by the so-called 'Social Contract' which lasted until July 1975. The current policy dates from 1 August 1975 and is called 'the attack on inflation' or, more commonly, 'Social Contract Mark II'. These latter three policies are set out in detail in the sections below.

The Social Contract

The Social Contract evolved during the latter months of 1974 as a result of discussions held between the government and the T.U.C. concerning the vacuum left by the termination of Phase III. The emphasis was placed firmly upon the principal of voluntary compliance since the unions remained wedded to the principle of free collective bargaining and the government did not wish to alienate its main source of support. The Social Contract contained two main provisions on the wages front. In the first place, pay awards were not to be permitted at intervals of less than one year from the previous award, and in the second place pay awards were to be geared to the rate of price inflation such that, over the period of the pay agreement, gross money wages (rather than disposable income) were to rise at the same rate as prices. On the prices front the regulations governing Phase III remained substantially unchanged although the government recognised the need to avoid any further erosion of the already serious shortage of liquidity in the company sector.

The Social Contract was deliberately left rather vague since the T.U.C. preferred it that way, and hence provided a good deal of scope for groups such as the miners to exceed its stipulations on pay by claiming exemption as 'special cases'. However, as the months passed the number of 'special cases' grew alarmingly and the rate of wage inflation rose to over 30 per cent, a figure which put paid once and for all to the notion that the Social Contract would hold down wages. Additionally, the government introduced the stipulation that the nationalised industries should make a surplus wherever possible, and the inevitable response was a rapid and unparalleled increase in the prices of fuel, transport and postal services.

The Attack on Inflation

The realisation that the Social Contract was not working as well as had been hoped was widespread by mid-1975. On 9 July the T.U.C. General Council issued a statement entitled 'The Development of the Social Contract'. In this statement they recommended the adoption of a flat-rate approach, fixing the pay limit at 10 per cent in order to give £6 a week to all full-time adult workers earning less than £7000 per annum. Above this cut-off point a pay freeze was recommended. They also recommended that the twelve-month interval between pay awards should continue to apply. On 11 July the government published a White Paper entitled 'The Attack on Inflation'.[3] Its main provisions were as follows:

(1) The target rate of inflation was to be an annual rate of 10 per cent by the late summer of 1976, and of less than 10 per cent by December 1976;

(2) A limit of £6 was to be imposed on all pay awards. This £6 was to be a maximum within which negotiations would take place. It was recognised that not all employers would be able to afford it;

(3) The upper income limit for the £6 increase was set at £8500 per annum;

(4) The restraint on incomes was to be by consent of the interested parties. The government was opposed to criminal sanctions and did not favour detailed intervention in collective bargaining;

(5) Increases in dividends would be limited to 10 per cent per annum, and the charges and profits of the self-employed would continue to be subject to price controls;

(6) The rate-support grant payable to local authorities would be restricted so that if there was any national pay settlement in excess of the limit, no grant would be payable on the excess. In addition the government would be prepared to use its powers of control over local-authority borrowing, including access to the capital market, to reduce the capital programmes of particular local authorities if this proved necessary to offset any excess expenditure on pay settlements;

(7) The government would not foot the bill for excessive settlements

in the nationalised industries through subsidies by permitting extra borrowing, or by allowing excess costs to be loaded on to the public through increased prices or charges;

(8) The government would not allow firms which made excessive pay settlements to reflect these settlements in higher prices to the consumer. With every application to the Price Commission for a price increase employers would have to notify details of any pay settlement underlying the application and the government would certify to the Commission whether any of these settlements exceeded the limit. Where an employer broke the pay limit, the whole pay increase would be disallowed for price increases;

(9) If the government found that the policy needed to be enforced by applying a legal power of compulsion, they would introduce such a power. Legislation had already been prepared which, when applied in particular cases, would make it illegal for an employer to exceed the pay limit;

(10) The government would continue the present strict price control enforced by the Price Commission under the price code. The government did not, however, intend to push price control to the point where it would endanger employment and investment.

(11) Price restraint would in due course be introduced on selected products of special importance in family expenditure, and food subsidies would also be increased;

(12) For 1976–7 the government proposed to limit rent increases so that rents would not rise faster than prices generally. This implied rent increases of only 60p per week in the Spring of 1976; and

(13) The government proposed to introduce a temporary employment subsidy which would not be available to companies which exceeded the pay limit.

What Type of Policy?

(i) Voluntary

It almost goes without saying that an essential ingredient of any prices-and-incomes policy is a high degree of co-operation from all affected parties. It is logical to assume that such co-operation is more likely to be forthcoming where the policy involves voluntary compliance rather than compulsion, and we will indeed discover in the section on effectiveness below that the only policy to have run its course with any degree of success was the voluntary policy of 1948–50.

In principle the ideal arrangement would be a voluntary agreement signed by the C.B.I. acting on behalf of employers and the T.U.C. acting on behalf of the unions, since this would eliminate the need for any interference by the authorities. Failing this the authorities should intervene to obtain publicly stated compliance from these two bodies that they will abide by certain rules laid down by the authorities. This was in fact what happened in 1948, in 1964 when both sides of industry signed a 'Declaration of Intent', and also in 1965 with the appearance of a voluntary early-warning system for prospective wage and price increases, and in 1974–5 during the life of the Social Contract. The great advantage of such compliance is not so much that it implies the existence of sanctions if the agreement is broken,[4] but that if either party to the agreement subsequently fails to meet its commitments the blame for the breakdown of the policy can be apportioned to the correct quarter. Also of course the government can absolve itself of all responsibility for subsequent price rises.

A voluntary policy cannot function, however, unless the signature of the parties to the agreement can be treated as binding upon their members. Unfortunately, whereas it is fair to say that the C.B.I. have a good record in this respect, as is evidenced by the price restraint exercised for six months in 1972, there continues to be a good deal of doubt about the ability of the T.U.C. to impose its will upon the individual unions which constitute its membership.

In this context it is worth bearing in mind that an individual worker is unlikely to see much benefit to himself from voluntary compliance with an incomes policy. Although he runs some risk of losing his job as part of the more general unemployment which normally goes hand in hand with rapidly escalating wages, he will tend to accept that risk in view of the considerable benefit to himself where he ends up as one of the lucky ones still in employment as against where everyone obtains the same mediocre pay award through compliance with the policy.

One way of making voluntary wage restraint more appealing to the worker is to offer him some kind of *guaranteed* increase in his *real* income. This can be done by resort to a *threshold agreement* which stipulates that if prices rise by more than the threshold amount during the course of the agreement then money wages must subsequently rise at the same rate as prices, thus preventing any further deterioration in real wages. This has the benefit of reducing workers' need to put in for substantial pay claims in the expectation that most of the benefits accruing therefrom will be wiped out by subsequent price rises, since any price rises which do occur above the threshold will automatically be reflected in higher money wages. This is a matter to which we will return in the subsequent chapter on indexation.

(ii) Public-sector controls

A half-way house towards a compulsory policy is the imposition of controls upon the public sector alone. In principle the government should be in a position to exert a great deal of pressure upon the public sector with respect both to prices and to incomes. It can, for example, refuse to authorise price increases for the nationalised industries, as it did in 1972 in order to keep public-sector prices in line with the C.B.I. proposals. It can also use its position as sole employer in the public sector to stand fast against excessive wage demands, as it did in 1961 and in 1970–1.

The idea behind such a policy is that the private sector is supposed to learn by example from the behaviour of 'employers' in the public sector. There are, however, good reasons to suppose that this tactic is no longer of any value, if, in fact, it ever was. In the first place the nationalised industries were given *carte blanche* in the Budget of April 1975 to raise prices in line with wage increases, and it is unlikely that this stipulation will be removed within the foreseeable future. In the second place public-sector pay awards have for the past year or more exceeded those in the private sector by a considerable margin. Once again it is difficult to foresee future administrations being able to face out the threat of strike action by mine workers or electricity workers denied pay awards commensurate with those being awarded to comparable private-sector workers.

(iii) Compulsory powers

The most repressive policy of all is a compulsory freezing of all incomes as from some specified date. This took place in 1966 and 1972, in each case following on from a substantial crisis which required a fairly radical short-term remedy. Experience suggests, however, that the passing of the crisis simultaneously removes the justification for the wage freeze, which means in practice that a freeze cannot be imposed for more than six months. This conclusion is borne out by the fact that whereas workers are willing to postpone their wage demands for a short time provided everyone is treated alike, anomalies and exceptions inevitably appear[5] to create inequities which become increasingly intolerable as time goes on. Also, since a freeze serves only to postpone wage demands rather than to adjust them in a downwards direction, there is little reason to expect that the catching-up process which occurs once the freeze is lifted will lead to anything other than the continuance of the long-term inflationary trend.

A rather shorter step along the road to compulsion is to introduce some kind of Prices-and-Incomes Board. The National Board for Prices and Incomes (N.B.P.I.) operated during the late 1960s under the chairmanship of Aubrey Jones, but was considered to be relatively ineffectual and was allowed to fade away.[6] Experience gained during the operation of this Board made it clear that its successors would need to have more extensive powers. The N.B.P.I. justifiably claimed in its final *Report*[7] that only the smaller and less important wage settlements were referred to it, whereas for the Board to prove influential it must make the decisions in those cases which are looked upon as providing an example for others to follow.

Partly because of the introduction of equivalent bodies in the United States during the preceding twelve-month period, the U.K. authorities established a Price Commission and a Pay Board in 1972 with more extensive powers than had been accorded to the N.B.P.I. Unfortunately, insufficient attention was given once again to the problem of implementation of these bodies' decisions, particularly in the context of a strike called in protest against a Pay Board ruling with the result that their authority was undermined.

It is widely accepted that, in principle, the ruling of a Pay Board ought to have the backing of the law. But, in practice, strikes are not illegal, and available sanctions are strictly limited even where the law is broken in some way, since imprisonment serves only to create martyrs. This tends to suggest that the Board cannot function effectively by threatening those who do not comply with its rulings with legalistic sanctions. Much more important in practice is the need to convince the working population that the Board exists to promote the pursuit of equity amongst different groups, a need which could be partly met by the implementation of a system of measuring pay relativities.

But at the end of the day it seems that there are a set of rocks on which all prices-and-incomes policies founder irrespective of the degree of compulsion involved. Prominent amongst these are the problems of evasion, exemption, and 'the norm'.

Evasion

The term 'incomes policy' is rather imprecise. Quite clearly it is easy to control money wages where people are paid weekly at time rates on P.A.Y.E. forms. But what about workers on piece rates, the payment of overtime rates for work which could easily have been done in normal working hours, or non-wage benefits? Controls over the latter are clearly not going to be at all easy to establish, which means either that the policy won't work at all, or that it will work for some but not for others (probably the greater of the two evils). The ease with which previous incomes policies have been evaded indicates that a great deal of thought in any such policy must be given to the question of evasion.

Much the same strictures apply on the prices front. It is obviously a simple matter to control the price of a standard product such as a pound of sugar. But in many cases any attempt to restrict the price of a good will result either in a reduction of quality which cannot be detected by the consumer, or the product will be repackaged or redesigned, given a new name, and the price put up accordingly.

Exemption

In previous policies, wage increases have often been linked to productivity. As was pointed out in the Introduction wage increases can be permitted where productivity is rising without this necessitating price rises. Unfortunately, it is apparently an easy matter to produce the illusion of rising productivity when justifying higher wages even if, in reality, it is static.[8] There are also considerable difficulties in measuring productivity in certain occupations such as teaching and nursing. However, even in trades where productivity is directly measurable, disparities are bound to arise because of differences in the capital–labour ratio.

Rather interestingly one point which was overlooked during previous policies was that if gross money wages were permitted to rise at the same rate as productivity, then disposable income necessarily rose at a slower pace. Hence this criterion for exemption can only be described as something of a con-trick perpetrated by the authorities upon the work-force.

A further exemption commonly authorised in the past was for lower-paid workers, since a given percentage increase in their money wages would have been very small in absolute terms. Unfortunately, although this exemption had the backing of the T.U.C., individual unions often took umbrage in practice because differentials between the lower-paid grades and other grades were necessarily affected. This is not to argue that exemptions cannot be enforced, but it seems clear from past experience that they tend to be seen as divisive rather than fair in many quarters.

The Norm

Any exemptions granted must be related to the established norm for wage increases. Looking back we find that the norm for wage and price increases in 1948, 1956, 1961 and 1966 was 0 per cent. From 1962 to 1964, however, the criterion was that wages and prices should not rise faster than the average increase in productivity. In 1965 the estimated acceptable level on this basis was raised from $2\frac{1}{2}$ to $3\frac{1}{2}$ per cent, but exemptions were introduced for the two categories set out above and also in situations where labour mobility needed to be induced, or on the basis of fair comparison with other industries. In mid-1968, after a period of prices-and-incomes freeze, the norm was re-established at $3\frac{1}{2}$ per cent with the exemptions continuing in force. Between 1968 and 1972 no official norm was in force, and hence no exemptions were laid down. The unofficial wage norm, however, rose first to 5 per cent and then in 1971 to 7 per cent. In 1972 a ninety-day wage standstill was imposed followed in 1973 initially by a norm of £1 + 4 per cent and subsequently by a norm of 7 per cent. Price controls were also introduced as detailed below. The wage norm under the 'Social Contract' was that pay awards should not exceed the rate of price inflation; and, under the current policy, is a maximum of £6 per week for those earning less than £8500 per annum. The price restraints are as detailed above.

The norm chosen clearly has to bear a close relation to the existing rate of inflation. It is pointless to lay down a norm of 3 per cent if wage inflation is running at about 10 per cent p.a. because, among other reasons, it is probable that some groups will be due for a sizeable pay award just after the incomes policy is made law, and these groups are going to do their best to ensure that the policy does not work effectively. However, past experience shows clearly that the main drawback to the fixing of a norm is that everyone treats it as a minimum rather than as a maximum figure. Hence it would appear to be a good idea, should a norm ever need to be reintroduced, to assign it the lowest possible value given the circumstances of the time.

Prices vs Incomes Policy

There can be little doubt that organised labour will not co-operate with an incomes policy unless prices and profits are controlled in addition to wages. This suggests that any attempt to impose an incomes policy in isolation is certain to come to grief, a fact of which previous administrations have by no means been unaware. It is, however, sometimes suggested that the best way to ensure the co-operation of the unions is to control prices alone,[9] thus reducing the necessity for trade unions to put in for large pay awards in the expectation of future price rises. There are, however, two main drawbacks to this proposal. In the first place, if the experience of the response of organised labour to the 1972 C.B.I. price limitation is anything to go by, wage demands will not be downgraded in response to price restrictions. In the second place, profits will almost certainly be squeezed, perhaps to the point of no return, by cost increases of all kinds. Certainly the difficulties experienced by many firms while stages 2 and 3 of the Counter-Inflation policy were in operation tends to bear out this conclusion.

The 1972–4 Policy

The policy in operation between November 1972 and October 1974 is of particular interest in that it exemplifies the classic three-phase policy of the post-war era. Furthermore, it illustrates how the authorities tried to overcome, albeit unsuccessfully, some of the difficulties encountered in previous policies. It is therefore of value to outline its progress below.

The very rapid rise in prices during 1971 and 1972 made new action on the inflation front a political necessity. Once again the government, at that time the Conservatives under Mr Heath, turned to a prices-and-incomes policy for want of a better alternative, despite the outcry emanating from the Monetarists. To a large extent this decision was influenced by the introduction of the 'New Economic Policy' by President Nixon in the United States on 15 August 1971. The early stages of the U.S. policy, consisting of a ninety-day standstill, followed by the setting up of a Price Commission and a Pay Board, appeared to have achieved considerable success in holding down the rate of inflation.[10]

U.K. policy followed closely that adopted in the United States. The Counter-Inflation (Temporary Provisions) Act of 30 November 1972 imposed a ninety-day standstill on prices, charges for services, pay, dividends and rents. Phase I of the policy lasted until the end of March 1973, and its most prominent features were that (*a*) prices of fresh food and imported raw materials subject to seasonal or overseas influences were largely uncontrolled; (*b*) interest rates were allowed to fluctuate more or less freely; (*c*) salary increments were unaffected; and (*d*) dividends could not be raised above the level of the previous financial year.

The Counter-Inflation Act of March 1973 covered the ensuing three-year period and set up a Price Commission and a Pay Board. These bodies were formed to administer a price-and-pay code which stipulated that (*a*) firms could recover only up to one-half of any increase in their labour costs, allowance being made for differing labour-intensiveness between industries; (*b*) net profit margins for sales in the home market were not allowed to exceed their average level in the best two of the preceding five years; (*c*) price controls did not apply to fresh foods, imports, and exported goods and services; (*d*) the total amount of the annual cost of pay increases for any group of employees was limited to the sum resulting from the payment of £1 per week plus 4 per cent of the average pay bill for the group over the previous year, exclusive of overtime, with a maximum for any one individual of £250 per annum; (*e*) settlements had to occur at no less than twelve-monthly intervals;

and (*f*) dividends could not rise by more than 5 per cent per annum.[11]

Phase III, introduced in October 1973, stipulated (*a*) a new norm for wage increases of 7 per cent which was to apply to negotiating groups rather than to individuals; (*b*) lower-paid workers, however, could opt for a flat rate of £2·25 per week, which implied an increase of over 7 per cent for all groups of workers earning on average less than £32 per week; (*c*) in addition there was an extra 1 per cent made available for sorting out any anomalies, although these had to be justified before the Pay Board; (*d*) on top of this there were extra payments in the form of an increased London differential, increases in unsocial shift bonuses of up to 20 per cent above straight time pay, various merit increases, and one extra day's paid holiday on New Year's Day.

Perhaps the most important stipulation, in the event, was the introduction of a wage threshold set at 7 per cent. If the Retail Price Index rose by 7 per cent above its level in October 1973 within the ensuing twelve-month period, then workers were entitled to a 40 pence threshold payment plus an extra 40 pence for each percentage rise above 7 per cent during the designated period. This represented in practice approximately a 1·2 per cent wage rise on average for every 1 per cent price rise above the threshold.

At the same time price controls remained in force more or less as per Phase II, although firms either making losses or earning less than 8 per cent return on capital employed were not subject to these controls. The government believed that these controls, combined with an improvement in productivity of the order of 3 or 4 per cent, would ensure that the threshold was not crossed, at least until the end of the summer.[12] In the event the threshold was reached in April 1974, and by the time that the policy was terminated twelve threshold increments had become payable, amounting to £4·80 per week. In view of this the policy can hardly be accounted a great success.

Alternative Approaches

It has occasionally been argued that the 1972–4 policy had little chance of success because it consisted essentially of a rehash of previously discredited ideas. The past few years have witnessed a resurgence of unofficial variants upon a prices-and-incomes theme.[13] So far these ideas have found little favour with the authorities, in part because they all have their own peculiar drawbacks. However, Weintraub and Wallich's tax-based incomes policy,[14] which recommends that corporations should be permitted to give pay rises above the norm, but that if they do so they must pay a surcharge on the corporate income tax equal to some multiple of the wage increase in excess of the norm, does appear to have been adopted by the Liberal Party.

Effectiveness

Before we go on to consider the various studies which have been done on the effectiveness of incomes policy there are certain reservations to have in mind. First of all there is no unanimity of statistical method adopted by the various investigators. Hence the varying results which have been obtained are clearly biased by the methods used.[15] Nevertheless, we can reasonably assume that, provided they all point more or less in the same direction, the drawing of conclusions is in order.

Secondly we may note that the majority of studies have been based upon a distinction between 'policy-on' and 'policy-off' periods which requires that a decision has to be made for better or for worse as to what is meant by an incomes policy. It is obvious, for example, that an incomes policy operated between 1961 and 1962, but 1956 is a doubtful starter[16] and the period between mid-1967 and late 1972 could fall into either category according to inclination, since although there was no official policy in operation the government was clearly holding down wages and prices in the public sector and at one point, the C.B.I. instituted a voluntary six-month period of price restraint. Unfortunately this latter period witnessed the most rapidly escalating inflation of them all. Thus the fact that the various studies almost all provide an estimate of the effectiveness of incomes policy *averaged out* over a number of policy-on periods suggests that the results of up-to-date studies may not be strictly comparable unless they utilise the same policy-on periods.

Finally we may note that the studies have been conducted over differing time periods. This tends to be important because, for example, the original 1948 voluntary policy was by far the most successful. Thus studies which examine only the early attempts at incomes policy tend to be more favourably disposed towards it than studies which produce results averaged out over all but the latest policy.

The earliest studies done in the United Kingdom were by Brechling,[17] Smith,[18] and the Prices and Incomes Board.[19] Brechling covered the period 1948(I) to 1965(IV) and found that comparing the actual change in weekly wage rates during the policy-on periods with predictions based upon the policy-off periods produced the following results: (i) 1948–50: weekly wage rates reduced by over 2 percentage points per annum; (ii) 1961–2: reduction of 1 percentage point p.a.; (iii) 1964–5: reduction of 2 percentage points p.a.; and (iv) 1948–65: average reduction of 1·8 percentage points p.a.

Smith covered the period 1948(I) to 1967(II) and produced estimates of the impact of incomes policy upon weekly wage rates, hourly wage rates and hourly earnings with or without overtime. Some of his findings[20] were that (i) 1948–50: weekly wage rates reduced by 2 percentage points p.a.; (ii) 1956: no significant effect; (iii) 1961–2: weekly wage rates reduced by 1·7 percentage points p.a.; (iv) 1962–4: no significant effect; (v) 1965–6: weekly wage rates reduced by 1 percentage point p.a.; and (vi) 1966–7: weekly wage rates reduced by 1·3 percentage points p.a.

In all periods the effect upon hourly wage rates was of less significance than the effect upon weeky wage rates. He also noted that the evidence did not point to a statistically significant direct effect on either retail or wholesale prices in any of the periods of incomes policy.

The next two studies of interest were by Lipsey and Parkin[21] and Parkin.[22] Lipsey and Parkin studied the impact of incomes policy upon weekly wage rates between 1948(III) and 1968(II). They found that only between 1948 and 1950 was there a significant average downward pressure on wages (of the order of 1·8 percentage points p.a.). However, prices rose during the same period by 0·75 percentage points p.a. more than had been expected on the basis of policy-off experience so that more than one-third of the potential anti-inflation effect of the successful wage restraint was lost. They also found that during the sub-period 1967(I) to 1968(II) of the policy-on period 1964(III) to 1968(II) weekly wage rates rose by 2·5 percentage points p.a. more than had been predicted.

Of more interest perhaps was their observation that incomes policy had the effect of swinging the Phillips Curve around a fulcrum at about the 1·8 per cent unemployment level, such that the new curve lay *above* the Phillips Curve when unemployment was *heavy* but *below* it when unemployment was *light*. Hence the unemployment–inflation trade-off was seemingly worsened in the former case but improved in the latter by the introduction of an incomes policy.

The Parkin study confirmed the previous findings and laid stress upon incomes policies rather than other explanations as the cause of the broken Phillips Curve. Wallis[23] however is very critical of Lipsey and Parkin's methodology as are Godfrey,[24] Burrows and Hitiris,[25] Sumner[26] and Taylor.[27] Hence it cannot by any means be taken as proven that there is a crucial level of unemployment above which incomes policies will on average fail.

We may also note by way of summary that Wallis found the 1948–50 incomes policy to have been the only one which significantly affected wage rates, but that prices were held down by over 2 percentage points in 1956. Taylor, examining the period 1953–70, argued that incomes policy was quite ineffective except during 1966, 1968 and the first half of 1969 when it was at its most severe, but that, anyway, periods of successful restraint have always been followed by catching-up periods once the brakes have been released. And Hines[28] considered the 1948–50 policy to have been the only one which succeeded in holding down wage rates between 1948 and 1969.

Parkin, Sumner and Jones therefore conclude that with the exception of the 1948–50 experiment, incomes policy 'apparently has little effect either on the wage determination process or on the average rate of wage inflation'.[29] They also conclude that incomes policy makes little discernible impact upon prices.[30]

Experience of incomes policies introduced overseas also gives little cause for optimism. As Table 10.1 shows there is no significant association between the percentage change in labour costs and the presence or absence of an incomes policy. The Netherlands, despite a complex incomes policy, appears well above West Germany, Italy and Belgium in the ranking despite the fact that the latter three

TABLE 10.1 *Average annual percentage increase in unit labour costs, 1953–69*

France	4·2	Norway	3·2	Austria	2·4
Netherlands	3·8	United Kingdom	3·2	West Germany	2·3
Denmark	3·6	Ireland	2·7	Italy	2·1
Finland	3·4	Sweden	2·6	Belgium	1·5

SOURCE: *National Institute Economic Review* (Nov 1971) p. 41.

countries have not had recourse to such a policy. Blackaby concludes: 'Thus we can find no country where incomes policy has been an obvious success over the whole post-war period, although some policies have had visible success in particular countries at particular times. Most short-term wage or price freezes have been successful in stopping wage and price increases for a year or two, but their long term effect has been doubtful.'[31]

The main characteristic of these periods of success was that the trade-union movement was (*a*) willing to go along with the policy, and (*b*) had sufficient power to extend a good deal of control over the changes in wages and earnings negotiated. However, although it is quite possible that the right environment for successful restraint on incomes and prices may reappear in other countries, it now seems extremely unlikely that it will ever do so again in the United Kingdom.

Conclusions

In the light of the evidence discussed above there appears to be no way whatsoever in which one can see fit to recommend that a prices-and-incomes policy be used as the *primary* weapon of anti-inflationary policy. On the other hand, the possibility of utilising such a policy as a supplementary form of control is rather more debatable. Any policy with the ability to depress expectations has a place in an anti-inflationary package. In our previous chapter on expectations, however, we concluded that past policies have had a barely perceptible impact upon expectations. That this is so is by no means surprising when one considers how ineffective all past policies other than that of 1948–50 have been. Of course the act of imposing a prices-and-incomes policy may serve to depress expectations at the time. The evidence suggests, however, that the act of removing it serves to raise expectations back to the level which they would have attained had no policy been imposed. On the whole, therefore, I am not inclined to regard the existence or otherwise of a prices-and-incomes policy as a matter of any fundamental importance at the present time. If inflation is to be cured then the main solution lies elsewhere.

11 The Monetarist Prescription

The Monetarists' prescription for curing inflation largely, though not exclusively, revolves around the issue of controlling the money supply. In their view if inflation is to be slowed down, then people must be persuaded that prices will not rise as much as originally expected during the ensuing time period. The way in which expectations of price rises can be adjusted downwards works broadly as follows.

At some stage in the never-ending round of wage and price increases the authorities step in to restrict the growth of the money supply to a rate below that of money National Income. Initially there is no reaction for reasons set out in the section on time lags above, but eventually households discover that, although their cash balances are broadly unchanged, the general price level is continuing to rise, with the result that the real value of these cash reserves is continually falling. This is generally referred to as a 'real-balance' effect. In order to restore the real value of cash balances households cut back on consumption expenditure and increase their savings, since the alternative method of supplementing cash balances, namely borrowing from the banking system, is unavailable other than on a highly restrictive basis. Firms in their turn are affected by the ensuing downturn in demand. They may choose to react to this by keeping prices at their current levels, but in that event they must reduce output substantially and lay off part of the work-force. Alternatively, prices may be reduced in order to avoid a fall-off in sales, in which case with money wages still rising rapidly, profit margins are quickly squeezed and a liquidity crisis develops. The banking system is unable to provide further liquid resources so workers once again have to be laid off. Thus, in either event, redundancies occur, and unemployment continues to rise until enough people are out of work for the bargaining power of the trade unions to be undermined. Once this point is passed, wage claims are reduced, taking into consideration the change in expectations consequent upon the realisation that prices are no longer rising, and the wage–price spiral is set into reverse gear. In this way the growth rates of money wages and of prices are wound progressively downwards without any further unemployment proving necessary. Eventually the growth rate of prices will fall into line with the new growth rate in the money supply. Once this point is reached the real value of cash balances will be restored to their customary level, consumption will pick up again, and it will be possible to set the economy to rights without either excessive inflation or excessive unemployment.

It is immediately clear from the above that the initiating factor in the deflationary spiral is a reduction in the money supply, and that the main transmission mechanism is an increase in the level of unemployment above the natural rate. However, no permanent increase in unemployment is intended. Once inflation has been reduced to the desired level the level of employment will gradually revert back to its natural rate. However, this does raise the question as to the speed with which equilibrium can be restored. In this respect the overriding factor appears to be that the more rapidly is the rate of inflation reduced, the higher will be the average level of unemployment during the adjustment process. In other words, one can cure inflation quite quickly by means of a massive dose of unemployment – something along the lines experienced during the 1930s. Alternatively, one can cure inflation without recourse to levels of unemployment which are totally unacceptable from a policy point of view, provided the authorities are not in too much of a hurry. The precise quantitative nature of these options can only be estimated with considerable difficulty. Certainly, in the light of the numbers currently out of work, one must treat with extreme caution the estimates of 2–2½ per cent unemployment which are considered by the members of the Manchester Inflation Workshop to be all that is necessary for a gradual slowdown in inflation.

Control Over the Money Supply

If the rate of growth of the money supply is to be controlled then there are policy implications in both international and domestic spheres. In the former case the U.K. authorities must set out to isolate themselves from internationally generated money flows. This can be done through the introduction of a freely fluctuating exchange rate which serves to ensure that the balance of payments remains constantly at or near its equilibrium value of zero, thus avoiding either massive inflows or outflows of sterling. A 'managed' float of the currency such as is currently being operated by the U.K. authorities does not eliminate sizeable surpluses or deficits *per se*. However, the Bank of England can sterilise a substantial part of any capital inflow which might occur under a managed float via open-market operations and the adjustment of bank reserve requirements, provided that the exchange rate is not too far from its equilibrium value.

However, controls over the growth in the money supply must be directed primarily towards the domestic sector. Here a good deal of the brunt must fall upon the government itself, since it is the phenomenal growth in the public-sector borrowing requirement which accounts in good part for the very rapid growth in the money supply over the past seven or eight years. In 1969–70 public expenditure was running at approximately £20 billion per annum and there was no borrowing requirement to speak of during that period. Between March 1974 and April 1975 public expenditure rose to nearly £50 billion per annum, and the borrowing requirement rose from £2·7 billion to an incredible £10 billion, although the Budget measures of April 1975 were expected to reduce this by approximately £1 billion. Now this borrowing requirement can be funded in one of two principal ways. Either the money is forthcoming from the private sector who purchase gilt-edged stocks and National Savings, or from the banking sector. In the latter case the money supply is not greatly affected provided that bank lending to the public sector is offset by a corresponding reduction in bank lending to the private sector. However, a determined attempt to reduce the availability of credit to the private sector will have serious implications for corporate cash flows and investment plans and is therefore not to be recommended. It is possible that the private sector will be willing to finance even historically large borrowing requirements provided that interest rates are kept up at attractive levels. The general tendency for interest rates to fall concurrent with the massive rise in the borrowing requirement does suggest, however, that if the money supply is to be reduced substantially in the near future then public-sector spending must come under the proverbial axe.[1]

In principle, controls must also be exercised over bank lending to the private sector. Such lending has periodically accounted for a significant part of the increase in the money supply. However, this may have been directly affected by the public-sector borrowing requirement itself, since 'As the public sector absorbed, through its borrowing, a significant proportion of the private sector's financial resources, the need for the private sector to borrow on a large scale, from banks and other institutions, to supplement these resources inevitably increased.'[2]

Shifting the 'Natural Rate'

Aside from the question of indexation which has been assigned a chapter on its own (pp. 134–40), the other subsidiary element in the Monetarist prescription is the desirability of shifting the natural rate of unemployment to the left. As a result, that steady rate of inflation which will be attained in long-run equilibrium will be associated with a lower level of unemployment than before. The natural rate can be shifted to the left by any factors which serve to improve the functioning of the labour market generally, for example better information dissemination about available jobs and enhanced regional-policy incentives for firms.

12 Discretionary Demand Management

In its extreme version the Monetarist position requires that the money supply be increased at a constant rate year after year in line with the expected trend in the growth of money National Income. Although many of the Monetarists would prefer to conceive of controlling the money supply in a more flexible manner, this policy is necessarily rather slow to operate because of the time lags between originating a change in the money supply and the consequent impact upon expenditure. For this reason other commentators prefer to stick with the more traditional forms of demand management, whether fiscal or monetary, which operate with rather shorter time lags. Also, of course, many commentators feel rather unsure about the postulated link between the money supply and the price level, and prefer to place their faith in what they consider to be other well-proven methods of curtailing expenditure, such as increases in direct or indirect taxation.

Discretionary fiscal and monetary measures, like control over the money supply, operate upon the inflation rate via induced unemployment. If, to take one example, interest rates are raised and controls are imposed upon bank lending, the net effect will be to reduce consumption expenditure, thus causing consumer-good producers to lay off workers. Where, alternatively, the authorities raise either direct or indirect taxation rates, the net effect will be to reduce real disposable income with the same eventual impact upon employment. In either event the ensuing unemployment is expected to induce moderation in wage demands, and hence to reduce inflationary pressures.

In general, much more interest is expressed in discretionary fiscal measures than in discretionary monetary measures. This is due in part to the fact that the U.K. authorities have maintained a predominantly Keynesian outlook on the control of the economy during the post-war years, and in part because those commentators who regard monetary weapons as being more powerful than fiscal weapons tend to give priority to control over the money supply.

If we now concentrate upon fiscal measures then the fundamental point to have in mind is that during the 1960s orthodox fiscal policy was designed to mop up excess demand by increasing either direct taxation, indirect taxation, or both simultaneously. However, although it appears intuitively obvious that reducing inflation requires higher taxes, further thought suggests that precisely the opposite conclusion should be drawn.

Consider first indirect taxation. If the rate of V.A.T. is raised from 8 per cent to 25 per cent on luxury goods (as in the Budget of April 1975) then this causes an immediate upwards movement in the Retail Price Index because the prices of such goods are marked up accordingly. In other words, higher rates of indirect taxation are themselves inflationary in the short term. Their long-term impact depends upon the reaction of wage-earners to such changes in taxation. If they respond by putting in for wage increases which are pitched at a level designed to restore real disposable income to its previous level, and if such increases are granted, then the rate of inflation will again be boosted, this time from the wages side, although the original stimulus remains the tax change. By this line of reasoning, reductions in indirect taxation should cause wage-earners to lower their expectations of future price rises, and hence to reduce their wage demands accordingly. It is therefore quite plausible to argue that reducing inflation requires lower indirect taxes.

Much the same logic applies to changes in direct taxation. We have already pointed out that high rates of inflation combined with relatively static tax allowances and direct tax rates result in a redistribution to the authorities of an ever-increasing proportion of the total wage bill. This is because increasing numbers of wage-earners who initially pay no income tax rise above the tax threshold, and also because all those above the tax threshold are taxable at the marginal rate on all of their additional income.

Now if, as appears increasingly to be the case, workers bargain for a given increase in their *real disposable income* rather than in their real gross income, any increase in the proportion of income deducted at source is likely to lead to escalated wage demands in money terms by way of compensation. This being so it becomes clear that if there is a *reduction* in the rate at which direct taxation is levied then a given level of real disposable income is compatible with a *reduction* in the rate of growth of money wages, which in turn is compatible with a reduction in the rate of price inflation.

A policy of fiscal ease should, however, be combined with other measures for maximum effect. In this respect there is much to be said for the policy combination of tight control over the money supply taken in conjunction with a lowering of tax rates generally. Two provisos should be borne in mind, however, if this policy combination is to work. In the first place a policy of fiscal ease, unless it is accompanied by commensurate reductions in public expenditure, is likely to produce substantial Budget deficits. If these deficits are funded by borrowing from the banking system then the whole point of the monetary restraint will be lost because the authorities will lose control over the money supply once again. Such deficits must, therefore, be funded largely out of private and corporate savings. In the second place, in order to ensure that money-wage claims are reduced in the desired manner, workers must be educated to the fact that, from a real disposable income point of view, a tax cut is just as good as a wage rise. Provided that these two provisos are met then this policy combination has a considerable potential for success. Furthermore, the impact upon the level of employment is much less severe than the policy combination of a reduction in the money supply in conjunction with higher rates of taxation. Reduced levels of taxation should make investment a more attractive proposition, and there is no necessity for investment funds to be hard to come by, even if the money supply is under control, provided that less essential expenditure, whether by the household or government sector, is kept within carefully prescribed limits. Thus, although this policy combination should serve to keep demand in check, it should also promote investment expenditure and avoid heavy unemployment. The impact of this policy combination will be enhanced by cuts in public expenditure which will release resources for investment in the private sector, and simultaneously help restrain the money supply. Finally, indexation should be of some assistance in holding down expectations of future price rises in the manner described in the next chapter,

Subsidies

The Labour administration embarked in 1974 upon a policy of direct subsidisation of certain widely consumed foodstuffs such as milk and butter. Given that these products are important constituent elements of the Retail Price Index it is obvious that such subsidies serve to prevent the Index from rising as fast as it would otherwise have done. But given the expense to the Exchequer of providing these subsidies it is extremely questionable whether they perform a desirable role in the struggle against inflation. Prior to the Budget of November 1974 most nationalised industries also held their prices below free-market levels by government edict. This amounted to subsidisation by another name, and also served to hold down retail prices generally. Interestingly enough, although the government decided to terminate these subsidies at that time, food subsidies were not affected.

In the first place it is obvious that subsidies cannot affect the underlying trend in the inflation rate unless they are provided at an ever-increasing level, a possibility far too costly to contemplate. Yet if all they achieve is to affect relative prices, for example by lowering the price of butter as compared to that of margarine, demand for the subsidised goods may be stimulated to the point of creating scarcities or of diverting resources to the production of these goods from other more appropriate usages.

At the end of the day one suspects that the use of subsidies is more of a ploy designed to endear the authorities to the 'working-class' voter than a serious anti-inflationary measure.

Import Controls

Increasing support has been voiced recently, especially by the New Cambridge School,[1] for the reintroduction of import controls. Import controls serve in principle as a fairly crude method of protecting home employment in that they keep imported goods out of the home market, but by implication they also serve to increase unemployment elsewhere in the world. Such beggar-my-neighbour policies are hardly likely to enhance the United Kingdom's popularity with her overseas creditors and trade partners, so why are they being recommended?

The United Kingdom currently faces the problem of simultaneous rapid inflation and heavy unemployment. The Chancellor, not surprisingly, wishes to suppress inflation without creating any further unemployment. But according to the New Cambridge School there is a direct link between the size of the public sector borrowing requirement and the deficit in the balance of payments.[2] This being so an improvement in the payments balance can only be achieved via a reduction in the borrowing requirement, that is, by cuts in public expenditure which will themselves create further unemployment. It is argued, therefore, that what is needed is some method of creating employment without this entailing either an increase in the borrowing requirement or in the balance-of-payments deficit. Reflating the economy is clearly not a satisfactory solution, nor can a prices-and-incomes policy be expected to have much effect upon the level of employment until business confidence is restored. The only possibilities are exchange-rate changes or import controls. Since, however, exchange-rate depreciation serves to increase the price of imported goods whereas physical controls on imports do not, the New Cambridge School advocate the latter alternative rather than the former. Such controls, they go on to argue, must be directed primarily towards imports of manufactured goods since the United Kingdom appears to be well on the way to becoming a net importer of manufactures.[3]

Import controls, however, are by no means an ideal solution. Following their imposition there will be a switch from imports to home-produced goods, some of which would have otherwise been exported. As a result export sales are likely to decline thereby causing an offsetting deterioration in the balance of payments. The consequent expansion of import-substitute sectors of the economy is likely to produce labour-supply bottlenecks which can only be resolved by bidding up wages in order to attract more labour, and these higher wages will probably spread throughout the economy via the usual transmission processes of pay comparability. This, in turn, will raise wage costs in the exporting sectors and cause a further fall off in export sales. Finally, the strategy of import substitution will necessarily require additional imports of raw materials and semi-finished products. As a result the over-all effect upon the balance of payments, taking both the import and export sides of the equation into account, may be detrimental, although this is less likely to be true where the economy is operating with considerable excess capacity. Even in the latter case, however, much depends upon whether the right sort of workers are available to be drawn into import-substitute industries, and wages may be forced upwards even at times when there is widespread unemployment.

Import controls have been tried before although not generally in the form of physical import quotas. From 1964 to 1966 the United Kingdom operated a Temporary Import Charge initially of 15 per cent, falling to 10 per cent. An Import Deposit Scheme also operated from 1968 to 1970, but as with the T.I.C. its impact appears on recent evidence[4] to have been far less than the authorities originally envisaged. In view of this the detrimental effects which these policies had upon relations with the United Kingdom's trading partners may be considered a high price to have paid.

In preceding chapters we have argued the case for flexible exchange rates. By cheapening exports and raising the price of imports an exchange-rate depreciation increases employment in both export and import-substitute sectors. It is therefore more likely than import controls to effect an improvement in the balance of payments and to create additional employment. Furthermore, such a policy does not contravene the I.M.F. regulations on the conduct of trade. On the whole, therefore, the introduction of import controls does not appear to have much to recommend it at the present time.

13 Indexation

Over the past year or so increasing attention has been paid to the possibility of introducing indexation of economic variables, and especially of wage rates as a supplementary form of inflation control. This interest in indexation stems in part from the adoption of threshold agreements under Stage 3 of the Counter-Inflation Act, and in part from a growing feeling that inflation cannot be suppressed and that the best thing to do in the circumstances is to learn to live with it as best one can. Indexation currently forms a part of the Monetarist platform for inflationary control,[1] and has been widely advocated in its own right.[2] It is therefore necessary at this point to give the question of indexation careful consideration.

The object of the exercise in introducing indexation is to preserve the real value of economic variables which are customarily measured in money units. This is done by linking such variables to an index which can be used to convert them into real magnitudes, for example to the Retail Price Index. We can illustrate this proposition most clearly by considering some specific examples.

In the case of wages and salaries the objective is to ensure that negotiated increases in the recipients' standard of living are preserved throughout the period covered by the agreement. Such an agreement might, for example, stipulate a guaranteed increase in real wages of 5 per cent. Assuming that productivity is expected to improve at the rate of 5 per cent p.a. and that prices are expected to rise at 10 per cent p.a., the actual negotiated rise in money wages becomes 15 per cent. However, should prices rise more quickly than expected during the relevant time period then money wages are varied accordingly, rising by 1 per cent for each additional 1 per cent rise in the Retail Price Index in excess of 10 per cent. Thus, at the end of the agreement, the workers' real income has gone up by 5 per cent irrespective of the rate of price inflation.

Interest rates can also be indexed so that they yield a positive rate of return on savings. The agreement in this case stipulates the real rate of return, which on the basis of the expected annual rise in prices yields the appropriate nominal rate of return. Thus, if prices are expected to rise by 10 per cent p.a., a positive real rate of return of 5 per cent requires a nominal rate of return of 15 per cent. Furthermore, this latter figure is negotiated to rise by 1 per cent for each additional 1 per cent rise above 10 per cent in the Retail Price Index during the year. This principle can also be extended to incorporate the monthly repayment on mortgages. This latter variable can be held constant in real terms by increasing it in line with increases in average wage rates or earnings. Although this does result in extremely costly mortgages in money terms when wage inflation is rapid, the real burden of repayment is unaffected, and one should bear in mind that a mortgage currently costs approximately 8½ per cent p.a. net of tax at a time when wages are rising by 30 per cent p.a. and house prices on average by over 20 per cent p.a. In fact, the cheapness of mortgages is dependent upon depositors with Building Societies earning a negative real rate of return on their savings.

Another important area for indexation is the tax system. We have already noted that if both tax thresholds and tax rates are held constant in nominal terms, then inflation serves to redistribute an ever-increasing proportion of total earnings to the authorities. The object of indexing the tax system is to keep the proportion of earnings deducted more or less constant over time. One way of doing this is to link the tax threshold to the annual rate of change of earnings. which thereby ensures that an individual who begins below the tax threshold at the time of indexation remains so thereafter, even when earnings are rising rapidly.

Indexation is by no means a new concept and is referred to frequently in the neoclassical literature. It has also been introduced on a limited scale in many countries during the past fifty years. Page and Trollope set out to examine the results of indexation experienced in twenty-one relatively well developed economies,[3] including the

United Kingdom; in sixteen cases wages were indexed, in thirteen cases pensions or other forms of transfer payment, and in twelve cases some form of investment income or capital asset. No country has ever tried to introduce anything resembling a universal system of indexation.[4] The United Kingdom has indexed wages on two occasions, namely in the periods 1915–22 and 1973–4 (the threshold agreements). Developments are also in progress on two fronts. In the first place, the intention is to provide a basic state pension linked to increases in average earnings, and in the second place there are moves afoot to index small savings. It is, however, very debatable that these developments are the forerunners of a much more widespread use of indexed agreements, since the question of the desirability of such a move is by no means established (for reasons discussed below).

The past history of indexation unfortunately provides little assistance in assessing its benefits in the current crisis. Page and Trollope's own conclusion is that

> Indexing has not had a major identifiable effect on the economy in any of the countries studied. It does not appear to have had a significant effect on inflation either way. Sometimes it has been part of an incomes policy that has changed relative incomes but in itself it has had no more than a marginal redistributive influence which seems if anything to have favoured holders of capital rather than labour, with little effect on those receiving pensions or other welfare benefits. It does not seem to have had any consistent influence on the current account of the balance of payments or on external capital flows. Nor does it appear to have affected private saving, although in combination with other policies general indexation may have encouraged economic growth by reducing the element of uncertainty for potential investors.[5]

One must bear in mind, however, that the United Kingdom's current economic situation differs considerably from previous experience, and it may therefore be appropriate to examine afresh the pros and cons of indexation.

The really crucial issue is whether the thresholding of wage agreements is itself inflationary. In this respect it is necessary to make a distinction between full wage indexation and threshold agreements of the kind in force in 1974. Full wage indexation requires that the threshold be fixed at a zero rate of price inflation. If there is no price inflation at all then workers fail to obtain any increase in money wages at all. The norm is a zero real-wage increase all round. Workers are then entitled to a one per cent rise in money wages for each one per cent rise in the Retail Price Index. Full wage indexation is therefore another name for a real-wage freeze, although this must be distinguished carefully from a money-wage freeze of the kind introduced in the past, because with full wage indexation no worker's standard of living is actually eroded while the policy is in force, such as happens during a money-wage freeze. However, full wage indexation is a very stringent policy and it is fairly certain that it would have to be eased after the worst of the crisis is over, perhaps by allowing the norm to rise to a level dictated by the average rate of improvement in productivity at the time.

Now it is obvious that, in the first place, the introduction of full wage indexation cannot initiate an inflationary spiral. Under such a system money wages cannot rise at all unless prices have previously been forced upwards by some stimulus such as higher taxes. In the second place, such wage increases as do take place are not themselves inflationary since they serve only to compensate exactly for increases in prices which have already taken place. However, the same conclusion does not necessarily apply when one turns to consider threshold agreements of the looser kind such as that employed in 1974. Such an agreement, which fixes the threshold at some level well in excess of the rate of productivity growth, can affect the rate of inflation, although the net effect is unlikely to be of great consequence. Clearly, if the amount of compensation offered for each one per cent increase in the Retail Price Index is equivalent to an increase of more than one per cent in average earnings, then this will result in further upwards pressure upon prices independently of that already in existence. If, on the other hand, the trade unions agree to accept lower money wages in return for the real-income guarantee, and in the event the agreed threshold is not reached, then prices will not rise by as much as they would otherwise have done in circumstances in which trade-union wage demands seek not merely to compensate for previous price increases but for those which have yet to come. Over all, therefore, there seems to be a case for the introduction of some form of indexation of wages provided that the wage increase agreed for when the threshold is crossed does not over-compensate for the prior increase in the rate of price inflation.

Of course, if gross real wages are to be maintained, then there must be a very strong case in principle for simultaneous indexation of direct taxation in order that net real income should also be maintained. Indexing direct taxation does, however, imply that the distribution of the burden of taxation is regarded as equitable since it becomes institutionalised once indexation is introduced. As Allen and Savage point out 'If the existing distribution is not optimal then the case in favour of indexing becomes less clear, but it is doubtful whether the irregular pattern of redistribution produced through inflation will correspond closely to the changes desired by society.'[6] Indexation of direct taxation is not only desirable on grounds of equity but also has significant implications from the government's point of view since it will serve to slow down the rate at which taxation revenue increases. This should force the authorities to reconsider their planned expenditure and should also cause them to reconsider their general attitude towards rapid inflation. Of course, they could respond by raising tax rates so that, although wage-earners no longer cross tax thresholds, total tax revenue continues to rise. This must, however, be seen as an expedient of limited value given the high marginal rates of taxation already in force.

There are also strong grounds for indexing at least some kinds of interest-bearing deposits. In the first place it is clearly iniquitous that savings should earn a negative real rate of return. In the second place the possibility is ever present that the point may be reached at which households call it a day and go out to spend their available cash holdings. This would cause the flow of capital to the manufacturing sector to dry up and would make it impossible for the authorities to dispose of more than a small fraction of their issued securities to the private sector, leaving them no alternative but to increase the money supply, at least in the short term. Furthermore, a spending spree would itself cause prices to rise. Whether such a situation will ever transpire is by no means easy to predict, but the implications of widespread dissaving are clearly very serious.

In the light of the preceding chapter it is important to consider how indexation fits in with the Monetarist prescription for curing inflation. We have already noted that control over the money supply operates upon the price level via induced unemployment, and hence via expectations of a reduction in the rate of price inflation in the future. The benefits of indexation in circumstances where the policy of controlling the money supply has begun to bite have been expressed by Friedman as follows:[7]

> More important, indexation will shorten the time it takes for a reduction in the growth of total spending to have its full effect in reducing the rate of inflation. As the deceleration of demand pinches at various points in the economy, any effects on prices will be transmitted promptly to wage constraints, contracts for future delivery, and interest rates on outstanding long-term loans. Accordingly, producers' wage costs and other costs will go up less rapidly than they would without indexation. This tempering of costs, in turn, will encourage employers to keep more people on the pay-roll, and produce more goods, than they would without indexation. The encouragement of supply, in turn, will work against price increases, with additional moderating feedback on wages and other costs.
>
> With widespread indexation, in sum, firm monetary restraint . . . would be reflected in a much more even reduction in the pace of inflation and a much smaller transitory rise in unemployment. The success in slowing inflation would steel political will to suffer the smaller withdrawal pains and so might make it possible for the (monetary authorities) to persist in a firm policy.

What must be clearly understood from the above is that indexation cannot be viewed as a cure-all for inflation. Friedman's argument is that indexation would help reduce inflation by reducing the pressure for inflationary policies and by making anti-inflationary policies more palatable. In this respect indexation is more accommodative than causal. The prime mover in the reduction in the rate of inflation necessarily remains conscious government policy to reduce its borrowing requirement – a policy best achieved according to Monetarist dogma via reductions in the money supply. In the case of the Brazilian economy which is widely regarded as a good example of the successful implementation of indexation, the sharp decrease in the rate of inflation stemmed principally from the reduction in Budget deficits and the rapid growth rate of the economy.[8]

But if the impact of indexation is primarily accommodative, what objections can be raised against it other than that it is itself inflationary? – a view to which we do not subscribe for the reasons set out above. The other main objections to indexation are (1) that many non-indexed contracts will continue to exist long after the indexation of, say, certain fixed-interest securities issued by the government, hence creating inequities of treatment as between different groups of savers, (2) indexation is tantamount to an acknowledgement that inflation cannot be cured but can only be lived with, and (3) there is no satisfactory index of real purchasing power with the result that people will be quick to believe that they are being inadequately recompensed for rises in the cost of living. Of these various objections only the last can be said to be of any real importance, and the drawback of an imperfect index is surely outweighed by the main benefit of indexation which is that, when used in conjunction with policies designed to suppress inflation, it serves to mitigate many of the adverse effects which such a policy would otherwise produce.

Over the past few years, as we have seen above, a wide range of objections have been raised to the introduction of indexation. Without wishing to play these down unnecessarily I believe that the fundamental objection – that indexation, especially of wages, is itself inflationary – cannot be sustained except in the context of the sort of threshold agreement introduced in 1974. A properly formulated policy of indexation should have no seriously adverse effects and should be of benefit in the context of the current rapid inflation both because it reduces the inequities which are otherwise inevitably associated with it, and because, aided with alternative inflation-combating policies, it can alleviate some of the adverse effects which might otherwise have been produced.

14 Conclusion

I have argued in the course of this book that an effective cure for the current inflation requires a many-pronged attack consisting, *inter alia*, of flexible exchange rates; control over the money supply and over credit creation; reductions in direct and indirect taxation; cuts in public expenditure; improvements in labour-market institutions; and indexation. This may appear at first sight to be a rather complex and long-winded collection of policy measures, especially when considered in relation to the prices-and-incomes policy which so many public figures are apt to treat as the be-all and end-all of inflation control. But I am personally inclined to believe that inflation is a multi-causal phenomenon which cannot be cured through adherence to any one particular measure unless it is taken to excess – and measures taken to excess generally bring social and political upheaval in their wake.

Given the unprecedented levels of wage and price inflation currently in existence it seems clear that bringing inflation down to single figures will in all probability take several years to achieve, during which time unemployment must necessarily remain at an historically high level. There appears, however, to be no good reason for unemployment to remain above the million mark other than in the short term, provided that the policy combination recommended above is adhered to. Of course, at the end of the day, the Chancellor may find these policy recommendations politically unacceptable. That, however, remains a topic outside the scope of our analysis.

The reader may prefer to interpret the evidence contained in this book in other ways. This he is perfectly free to do since no one can justly claim that the issue of inflation and its control is a closed book. The important thing is that the nature of the various controversies is clearly understood and that they are judged by the reader strictly according to their merits. Then at least the debate over the appropriate response to the current inflation can take place in a more rational atmosphere than has generally been the case in past years.

Notes and References

Chapter 1

1. The *Department of Employment Gazette* contains figures for product groups such as fuel and light as well as a composite figure pertaining to the general price level.
2. So called to distinguish it from the special index relating to expenditure by pensioners.
3. Formerly known as the Cost of Living Advisory Committee. In January 1975 the committee recommended that the weights used in the Index should be based upon the pattern of household expenditure over the most recent twelve months for which figures are available as against the current usage of a three-year average.
4. Which is why the decision to construct a separate index for pensioners was taken. There are, however, no declared intentions to introduce a special index for company directors.

Chapter 2

1. See, for example, A. G. Hines, 'Inflation and Economic Growth', in *Conflicts in Policy Objectives*, ed. N. Kaldor, and *Barclays Bank Review* (Feb 1973) p. 6, where it is argued that for five of the original E.E.C. members 'a higher rate of price rise between 1960 and 1970 tended to correspond with a higher growth of G.N.P., the same also being true of the three new members but at a lower level'. N. Paldam in the *Swedish Journal of Economics* (Dec 1973) p. 425, argues, however, that 'In the long run there is no (or at most a weak) relation between price increases and real growth as regards G.N.P.'
2. H. Lydall, *Journal of the Royal Statistical Society*, Series A, vol. 122 (1959).
3. J. A. Brittain, *American Economic Review*, papers and proceedings (May 1960).
4. T. Lynes, *National Assistance and National Prosperity*.

5. D. Seers, *The Levelling of Incomes Since 1935.*
6. R. G. Allen, *Economica* (1958) pp. 14–25.
7. D. G. Tipping, *Applied Statistics*, vol. 19, no. 1 (1970) pp. 1–17.
8. J. Muellbauer, *Economic Journal* (Mar 1974) pp. 45–6.
9. See, for example, H. P. Miller, *Income Distribution in the U.S.* and E. C. Budd and D. F. Seiders, *American Economic Review*, papers and proceedings (May 1971).
10. E. C. Budd, *American Economic Review*, papers and proceedings (May 1970).
11. G. L. Bach and J. B. Stephenson, *Review of Economics and Statistics* (Feb 1974) p. 13.
12. Ibid, p. 2.
13. Ibid. p. 5.
14. A. Glyn and B. Sutcliffe, *British Capitalism, Workers and the Profit Squeeze*, p. 58. See also C. Clark, *Lloyds Bank Review* (Oct 1974) which reaches the same conclusions with respect to the United Kingdom, the United States and Australia.
15. *British Capitalism, Workers and the Profits Squeeze*, p. 65.
16. M. Paníc and R. E. Close, *Lloyds Bank Review* (July 1973).
17. Ibid. p. 30.
18. G. J. Burgess and A. J. Webb, *Lloyds Bank Review* (Apr 1974) p. 17.
19. F. Wilkinson and H. A. Turner, 'The Wage–Tax Spiral and Labour Militancy', in *Do Trade Unions Cause Inflation?*, ed. D. Jackson, H. A. Turner and F. Wilkinson, ch. 3.
20. Ibid. p. 80.
21. Ibid. p. 81.
22. M. A. King, *Economic Journal* (Mar 1975) p.40.
23. Ibid. p. 41.
24. Ibid. p. 46. That stock appreciation holds the key to a true assessment of profitability is an opinion shared by G. Meeks, *Oxford Bulletin of Economics and Statistics* (Nov 1974).
25. *National Institute Economic Review* (Nov 1971) pp. 20–2.
26. See p. 78–90 for a full discussion of inflation and international trade, which incorporates the fixed- versus fluctuating-exchange-rate controversy.
27. The value of exports is calculated by multiplying quantity sold by price. Given a rise in price, total value may either rise or fall depending upon the extent of the resultant fall-off in demand (known technically as the product's demand elasticity).

Chapter 3

1. See P. J. Curwen and A. H. Fowler, *Economic Policy*, ch. 3.
2. A. W. Phillips, *Economica* (Nov 1958).
3. Ibid. p. 283.
4. Ibid. p. 285.
5. Ibid. p. 283.
6. Ibid. p. 290.
7. M. Desai, *Economica* (Feb 1975) p. 4.
8. Phillips, *Economica* (Nov 1958) pp. 290–1.
9. Desai, *Economica* (Feb 1975) pp. 3–4.
10. Phillips, *Economica* (Nov 1958) pp. 283–4.
11. See, for example, D. Mackay and R. Hart, *Manchester School* (June 1974).

12. Desai, *Economica* (Feb 1975).
13. R. G. Lipsey, *Economica* (Feb 1960).
14. Ibid. p. 10.
15. Ibid. pp. 11–12.
16. Lipsey does not specify whether he refers to money wages or real wages.
17. These being the micro market equivalents of the macro market *W* and *U*.
18. Lipsey, *Economica* (Feb 1960) p. 21.
19. Ibid. pp. 22–3
20. Ibid. p. 23.
21. Ibid. p. 24.
22. Ibid. p. 30.
23. R. G. Lipsey, *An Introduction to Positive Economics*, p. 711.
24. A fair cross section of these is to be found in the Bibliography. Broadly speaking any article which appears in the Bibliography but which is not referenced elsewhere in the text, falls within this category.
25. For example in J. Burton, *Wage Inflation*, and C. Mulvey and J. A. Trevithick, *The Economics of Inflation*.
26. D. W. Laidler, 'The Phillips Curve, Expectations and Incomes Policy', in *The Current Inflation*, ed. H. G. Johnson and A. R. Nobay, ch. 5, p. 78.
27. Lipsey, *Economica* (Feb 1960) p. 17.
28. Ibid. p. 31.

Chapter 4

1. See J. Taylor, *Unemployment and Wage Inflation*; 'Incomes Policy, the Structure of Unemployment and the Phillips Curve: the United Kingdom Experience, 1953–70', in *Incomes Policy and Inflation*, ed. M. Parkin and M. T. Sumner; *Southern Economic Journal* (July 1970); and L. Godfrey and J. Taylor, *Oxford University Bulletin of Economics and Statistics* (Aug 1973).
2. J. Taylor, *Economic Journal* (Dec 1972) p. 1363. For further evidence on the shake-out hypotheses see Taylor, *Unemployment and Wage Inflation*, pp .80–3; D. I. Mackay, *Oxford Economic Papers* (Mar 1972); D. Gujarati, *Economic Journal* (Dec 1972); and G. J. Evans, *Economic Journal* (Mar 1975).
3. P. G. Saunders, *Bankers* (May 1973).
4. D. Gujarati, *Economic Journal* (Mar 1972). See also J. K. Bowers, P. C. Cheshire and A. E. Webb, *National Institute Economic Review* (Nov 1970); and D. I. MacKay and G. L. Reid, *Economic Journal* (Dec 1972).
5. Taylor, *Unemployment and Wage Inflation*, p. 87, and in *Incomes Policy and Inflation*, ed. Parkin and Sumner, p. 190. He assumes payment at time and a half for overtime work.
6. Taylor, in *Incomes Policy and Inflation*, p. 197.

Chapter 5

1. Popular journalists have tended to devote much more space to the trade-union issue than to the money-supply controversy, not least because its exposition does not require of them a sophisticated knowledge of

economic theory. On the other hand, economics journals have devoted much more space to the money-supply controversy than to any other inflation-related topic.

2. There is, for example, another controversy currently being waged between Keynesians with respect to what Keynes really said, or meant to say, in *The General Theory*.

3. For further details see Curwen and Fowler, *Economic Policy*, ch. 3.

4. This formulation of the Quantity Theory is associated in particular with the work of Irving Fisher in, for example, *The Purchasing Power of Money*.

5. The expression *PT* should not, however, be confused with National Income because *T* includes all intermediate transactions as well as final transactions whereas National Income comprises only the latter.

6. In this case the two sides of the equation may or may not be equal to one another depending upon the respective values of the four variables at any given time.

7. In this case the two sides of the equation must *invariably* be equal to one another.

8. *T* would also tend to increase steadily over time as a result of increases in industrial capacity and hence in employment.

9. *V* was thought to be dependent upon habits, institutional arrangements and banking practices which are not subject to much variation over time. Obviously changes in these variables do cause *V* to fluctuate over time, but very little variation was expected in the short term with which the Quantity Theory was concerned.

10. All major trading nations operated for most of the period on a gold exchange standard which survived until 1931.

11. Attempts to apply the logic of neoclassical analysis to the U.K. economy during the early 1920s led to the General Strike in 1926. The trade unions, regrettably for the authorities, turned out not to be confirmed neoclassicists.

12. J. M. Keynes, *A Treatise on Money*.

13. J. M. Keynes, *The General Theory of Employment, Interest and Money*.

14. *PY* and *PT* are not, however, identical terms. This is because *T* measures the total number of transactions, whether intermediate or final, per time period, whereas *Y*, known as *real* National Income, measures the *real value* of final goods and services only. In this formula *V* becomes the *income* velocity of circulation.

15. For the sake of brevity it is necessary to assume at this point that the reader is conversant with the rudiments of Keynesian economics.

16. Known technically as the *marginal propensity to consume* and the *marginal propensity to invest* respectively. These expenditure decisions apply to goods and services produced in both domestic and foreign economies.

17. *Radcliffe Committee on the Working of the Monetary System*.

18. M. Friedman (ed.), *Studies in the Quantity Theory of Money*.

19. Mostly individuals, but for several years now Monetarism has been openly espoused by the Federal Reserve Bank of St Louis which has developed a model which lends empirical support to Monetarist doctrine. See the various articles cited in the bibliography credited to the *St Louis Review* and also D. M. Bechter, *Federal Reserve Bank of Kansas City Monthly Review* (July–Aug 1973).

20. For further details see, for example, A. Bain, *The Control of the Money Supply*, pp. 80–3.

21. Discretionary in the sense that such measures can be either introduced or relaxed at the discretion of the authorities.

22. Many of these revolve around the methodology and econometric techniques used by the New Quantity Theorists. These do not fall within the scope of this book but the interested reader is referred to the bibliography which contains the relevant source material. A particularly swingeing attack on Monetarism is to be found in A. G. Hines and C. Nussey, *Discussion Paper No. 23*, Birkbeck College (Apr 1974).

23. See, for example, Friedman's various works; C. A. Sims, *American Economic Review* (Sep 1972) or D. Laidler, *Manchester School* (Dec 1973) p. 388.

24. See, for example, P. Davidson and S. Weintraub, *Economic Journal* (Dec 1973) p. 118, and Hines and Nussey, *Discussion Paper No. 23*, Birkbeck College (Apr 1974).

25. This problem has been the subject of widespread commentary. See, for example, the *Bank of England Quarterly Bulletin* (June 1973); Bain, *The Control of the Money Supply*, p. 84; D. Kern, *National Westminster Bank Review* (Nov 1972); P. Wood and J. Rhys, *Bankers' Magazine* (Apr 1971); A. A. Walters, *Money in Boom and Slump*, and J. Waters, *National Westminster Bank Review* (Nov 1969).

26. Originally three sets of data were published – hence the missing M_2. M_2 is, however, in widespread use for analytical purposes in the United States.

27. A full explanation can be found in the *Bank of England Quarterly Bulletin*, vol. IX (1969) pp. 363–81, and also in the *Banker* (Jan 1975) pp. 17–21.

28. See, for example, A. A. Walters, *Bankers' Magazine* (Feb 1970).

29. See, for example, the *Banker* (Jan 1975) p. 27.

30. We will return to this question shortly. For a detailed discussion of this rather complex issue, see, for example, the *Bank of England Quarterly Bulletin* (June 1973) pp. 193–202, or Wood and Rhys, *Bankers' Magazine* (Apr 1971).

31. As is the view of Waters, *National Westminster Bank Review* (Nov 1969).

32. M. Friedman, *American Economist* (Spring 1972).

33. Walters, *Bankers' Magazine* (Feb 1970).

34. Walters, *Money in Boom and Slump*, p. 50.

35. This conclusion is, however, strongly disputed by Waters in the *National Westminster Bank Review* (Nov 1969).

36. See, for example, C. R. Barrett and A. A. Walters, *Review of Economics and Statistics* (Nov 1966).

37. Bain, *The Control of the Money Supply*, pp. 91–4, 88–91, 94–5 respectively.

38. M.Friedman, *Federal Reserve Bank of St Louis Review* (Mar 1974) p. 21.

39. See, for example, F. Modigliani, *Journal of Political Economy* (June 1964).

40. *Bank of England Quarterly Bulletin* (June 1973) pp. 200–1.

41. See, for example, M. Bronfenbrenner, *Journal of Political Economy* (Feb 1961); Modigliani, *Journal of Political Economy* (June 1964); and V. Argy, *Journal of Money, Credit and Banking* (Feb 1971).

42. See, for example, Waters, *National Westminster Bank Review* (Nov 1969); D. Laidler, *Bankers' Magazine* (Oct 1971); M. Artis, *Bankers' Magazine* (Oct 1972 and Nov 1972); and D. Tucker, *Journal of Political Economy* (Apr 1963).

43. Outstanding balances owed by the government to members of the nation from whom it has borrowed in order to bring its income into line with its expenditure.

44. But see, for example, Bain, *The Control of the Money Supply*, pp. 41–58.

45. As is, for example, the opinion of D. C. Rowan, *Manchester School* (Mar 1973).

46. *Bank of England Quarterly Bulletin* (June 1971).

47. See Waters, *National Westminster Bank Review* (Nov 1969) pp. 29–30.

48. See A. F. Burns, *Federal Reserve Bank of St Louis Review* (Nov 1973).

49. See, for example, M. Friedman, *Journal of Political Economy* (Oct 1961 and Oct 1969), J. M. Culbertson, *Journal of Political Economy* (Oct 1961); A. Ando and E. C. Brown, 'Lags in Fiscal Policy' in *Stabilization Policies*; T. Mayer, *Western Economic Journal* (Sep 1967); W. E. Gibson, *Quarterly Journal of Economics* (May 1970); M. Willes, *Federal Reserve Bank of Philadelphia Review* (Mar 1968); and M. J. Hamburger, *Federal Reserve Bank of New York Review* (Dec 1971).

50. Some economists have even gone on record with the suggestion that there is no longer any discernible trade cycle at all. See, for example, F. W. Paish, *Lloyds Bank Review* (Oct 1970). For a more contentious analysis of the whole trade-cycle issue see G. Sirkin, *Lloyds Bank Review* (Apr 1972).

51. See, for example, H. G. Johnson, *Inflation and the Monetarist Controversy*; L. C. Andersen and K. M. Carlson, *Federal Reserve Bank of St Louis Review* (Apr 1970); and M. W. Keran, *Federal Reserve Bank of St Louis Review* (Nov 1969).

Chapter 6

1. See, for example, E. S. Phelps, *Economica* (1967), 'Money Wage Dynamics and Labour Market Equilibrium', in *Microeconomic Foundations of Employment and Inflation Theory*, ed. E. S. Phelps *et al.*, and 'Inflation, Expectations and Economic Theory', in *Inflation and the Canadian Experience*, ed. N. Swan and D. Wilton; M. Friedman, *American Economic Review* (Mar 1968); R. E. Lucas, Jr and L. A. Rapping, *American Economic Review* (June 1969); S. J. Turnovsky and M. L. Wachter, *Review of Economics and Statistics* (Feb 1972); S. J. Turnovsky, *Journal of the American Statistical Association* (Dec 1970); D. Laidler, 'The Phillips Curve, Expectations and Incomes Policy', *The Current Inflation*, ed. H. G. Johnson and A. R. Nobay, ch. 5; Laidler, *Economica* (Feb 1973); Laidler, *Manchester School* (Dec 1973); A. Cukierman, *Econometrica* (Nov 1974); M. Parkin, M. T. Sumner and R. A. Ward, 'The Effects of Excess Demand, Generalized Expectations and Wage–Price Controls on Wage Inflation in the U.K.', *University of Manchester, mimeo 74/02* (Jan 1974); and J. A. Carlson and M. Parkin, 'Inflation Expectations', *University of Manchester, mimeo 73/05* (June 1973).

2. For a discussion of this issue see, for example, P. G. Saunders and A. R. Nobay, 'Price Expectations, the Phillips Curve and Incomes Policy', *Incomes Policy and Inflation*, ed. M. Parkin and M. T. Sumner.
3. Turnovsky and Wachter, *Review of Economics and Statistics* (Feb 1972).
4. The same data was later used by W. E. Gibson in the *American Economic Review* (Dec 1972).
5. Carlson and Parkin, 'Inflation Expectations'.
6. Turnovsky, *Journal of the American Statistical Association* (Dec 1970) p. 1442.
7. Carlson and Parkin, 'Inflation Expectations', pp. 19–20.
8. Such a mechanism is tested in, for example, R. M. Solow, *Price Expectations and the Behaviour of the Price Level*; J. M. Parkin, *Economica* (Nov 1970); and Saunders and Nobay in *Incomes Policy and Inflation*, ed. Parkin and Sumner.
9. Carlson and Parkin, 'Inflation Expectations', p. 17. This is known as a 'second-order' mechanism.
10. Ibid. p. 20.
11. Ibid. p. 33.
12. See Parkin, Sumner and Ward, 'The Effects of Excess Demand, Generalized Expectations and Wage–Price Controls on Wage Inflation in the U.K.', pp. 7–13, for a full exposition of a model of the determinants of changes in real wages.
13. See, for example, Solow, *Price Expectations and the Behaviour of the Price Level*; Cukierman, *Econometrica* (Nov 1974); Parkin, *Economica* (Nov 1970); A. Marin, *Three Banks Review* (Dec 1972); H. G. Johnson, 'Recent Developments in Monetary Theory: A Commentary', in *Money in Britain 1959–1969*, ed. D. R. Croome and H. G. Johnson, and especially A. Rees, *Economica* (May 1970).
14. See, for example, Friedman, *American Economic Review* (Mar 1968); Phelps, *Economica* (Aug 1967); Francis, *Federal Reserve Bank of St Louis Review* (Aug 1974); and Parkin, Sumner and Ward, 'The Effects of Excess Demand, Generalized Expectations and Wage–Price Controls on Wage Inflation in the U.K.'
15. See Parkin, *National Westminster Bank Review* (May 1974) p. 38.
16. See Mulvey and Trevithick, *The Economics of Inflation*, ch. 7.
17. See, for example, *National Institute Economic Review* (Feb 1971) p. 38.
18. *Midland Bank Review* (Nov 1974) p. 13.
19. Parkin, Sumner and Ward, 'The Effects of Excess Demand, Generalized Expectations and Wage–Price Controls on Wage Inflation in the U.K.'
20. Ibid. p. 7.
21. Ibid. p. 25.
22. C. J. Bruce, *Economic Journal* (June 1975).
23. Ibid. p. 374.

Chapter 7

1 For reasons explained by M. Whitman, *Journal of Money, Credit and Banking* (Nov 1969).
2. T. Congdon, *National Westminster Bank Review* (Feb 1973).
3. Ibid. p. 16.
4. O.E.C.D., *Economic Outlook* (July 1973) p. 86.

5. Ibid. p. 88.
6. H. G. Johnson, *Inflation and the Monetarist Controversy*, p. 85.
7. N. Duck, M. Parkin, D. Rose and G. Zis, 'The Determination of the Rate of Change of Wages and Prices in the Fixed Exchange Rate World Economy, 1956–1970', *University of Manchester, mimeo, 74/04* (Mar 1974).
8. Ibid. p. 7.
9. Except where the authorities are able to neutralise the entire addition to the reserves via, for example, open-market operations.
10. Devaluation of sterling in 1967 and of the French franc in 1958 and 1969; revaluation of the German mark in 1961 and 1969 and of the Dutch guilder in 1961.
11. Countries did, of course, have access to reserves held at the International Monetary Fund to tide them over short-term difficulties.
12. Duck, Parkin, Rose and Zis, 'The Determination of the Rate of Change of Wages and Prices in the Fixed Exchange Rate World Economy', p. 2.
13. D. Laidler, *National Westminster Bank Review* (Nov 1972) p. 31.
14. See, for example, W. Nordhaus, *Brookings Papers on Economic Activity*, no. 2 (1972) p. 459.
15. Duck, Parkin, Rose and Zis, 'The Determination of the Rate of Change of Wages and Prices in the Fixed Exchange Rate World Economy', pp. 30–1.
16. Nordhaus, *Brookings Papers on Economic Activity*, no. 2 (1972) p. 459.
17. See F. Machlup, 'World Inflation: Factual Background', in *Inflation As A Global Problem*, ed. R. Hinshaw, p. 29.
18. Ibid. pp. 27–8.
19. See table 1 in H. N. Goldstein, *National Westminster Bank Review* (Nov 1974) p. 18.
20. O.E.C.D., *Economic Outlook* (July 1973) pp. 89–90.
21. That is including speculative capital movements between currencies.
22. Duck, Parkin, Rose and Zis, 'The Determination of the Rate of Change of Wages and Prices in the Fixed Exchange Rate World Economy'.
23. Nordhaus, *Brookings Papers on Economic Activity*, no. 2 (1972).
24. Goldstein, *National Westminster Bank Review* (Nov 1974).
25. Ibid. p. 21.
26. See the *Federal Reserve Bulletin* (Oct 1974) table A60.
27. For a discussion of the role played by Eurodollars see R. Hinshaw (ed.), *Inflation As a Global Problem*, chs 3, 6.
28. O.E.C.D., *Economic Outlook* (July 1973) p. 90.
29. A view which is associated most closely with the Manchester University Inflation Workshop.
30. This being the view of the O.E.C.D. itself.
31. Goldstein, *National Westminster Bank Review* (Nov 1974) p. 23.
32. See ibid. table IV.

Chapter 8

1. The clearest exposition of the history of collective bargaining is to be found in the work of G. H. Phelps-Brown. See, for example, *British Journal of Industrial Relations* (Nov 1973).

2. Ibid. p. 334.
3. P. Wiles, *Economic Journal* (June 1973).
4. Ibid. p. 392.
5. Ibid. p. 382.
6. Ibid. p. 392.
7. C. Mulvey and J. Trevithick, *Economic and Social Review* (Jan 1973).
8. See D. L. Purdy and G. Zis, 'On the Concept and Measurement of Trade Union Militancy', in *Inflation and Labour Markets*, ed. D. Laidler and G. Purdy, ch. 2, p. 47.
9. L. A. Dicks-Mireaux and J. C. R. Dow, *Journal of the Royal Statistical Society* (1959).
10. R. Lipsey and M. Steur, *Economica* (May 1961) is the principal study based upon U.K. data. Evidence relation to the U.S. economy is summarised in Burton, *Wage Inflation*, pp. 45–8.
11. A. Hines, *Review of Economic Studies* (Oct 1964), *Economic Journal* (Mar 1969), and 'The Determinants of the Rate of Change of Money Wage Rates and the Effectiveness of Incomes Policy' in *The Current Inflation*, ed. Johnson and Nobay, ch. 8.
12. See, for example, D. L. Purdy and G. Zis, 'Trade Unions and Wage Inflation in the U.K.', in *Inflation and Labour Markets*, ed. Laidler and Purdy, chs 2, 3; R. K. Wilkinson and B. Burkitt, *Scottish Journal of Political Economy* (June 1973); L. Godfrey, 'The Phillips Curve: Incomes Policy and Trade Union Effects', *The Current Inflation*, ed. Johnson and Nobay, ch. 6; Mulvey and Trevithick, *Economic and Social Review* (Jan 1973); and Burton, *Wage Inflation*, pp. 55–7.
13. Purdy and Zis in *Inflation and Labour Markets*, ed. Laidler and Purdy, p. 51.
14. See, for example, Godfrey, in *The Current Inflation*, ed. Johnson and Nobay, ch. 6; Godfrey and Taylor, *Oxford Bulletin of Economics and Statistics* (Aug 1973); Taylor, in *Incomes Policy and Inflation* ed. Parkin and Sumner, ch. 10; and Taylor, *Unemployment and Wage Inflation.*
15. See, for example, R. Bean and D. A. Peel, *Journal of Economic Studies* (Nov 1974); H. Grossman, *Bankers' Magazine* (June 1971); Purdy and Zis, in *Inflation and Labour Markets*, ed. Laidler and Purdy, ch. 2; R. Ward and G. Zis, *Manchester School* (Mar 1974).
16. Bean and Peel, *Journal of Economic Studies* (Nov 1974) p. 89.
17. However, much of the blame for the recent inflation must be placed at the door of the coal mining union if trade unions in general are considered to be the cause of inflation. Most studies of union militancy exclude this industry because of its dominating, and sometimes perverse, influence on the over-all statistics.
18. Purdy and Zis in *Inflation and Labour Markets*, ed. Laidler and Purdy, p. 48. The method of calculation of the official statistics on strike activity is set out in each edition of the *Department of Employment Gazette*.
19. Ibid. p. 54.
20. See, for example, J. F. Goodman, *International Labour Review*, vol. 95 (1967).
21. See, for example, Ward and Zis, *Manchester School* (Mar 1974) p. 47.
22. Grossman, *Bankers' Magazine* (June 1971) p. 285. See also Congdon, *National Westminster Bank Review* (Feb 1973) and Laidler, *National Westminster Bank Review* (Nov 1972) p. 15 for further support for the expectations hypothesis.

23. Purdy and Zis in *Inflation and Labour Markets*, ed. Laidler and Purdy, p. 53. See also Marin, *Three Banks Review* (Dec 1972).

24. Purdy and Zis in *Inflation and Labour Markets*, ed. Laidler and Purdy, p. 58.

25. Ward and Zis, *Manchester School* (Mar 1974).

26. See, for example, F. P. R. Brechling, 'Wage Inflation and the Structure of Regional Unemployment', *Inflation and Labour Markets*, ed. Laidler and Purdy, ch. 7; J. D. Sargan, 'A Study of Wages and Prices in the U.K. 1949–1968', *The Current Inflation*, ed. Johnson and Nobay, ch. 4; O. C. Ashenfelter, G. E. Johnson and J. H. Penceval, *Review of Economic Studies* (Jan 1972); C. Mulvey and J. A. Trevithick, *Scottish Journal of Political Economy* (Feb 1974); O. Eckstein and T. A. Wilson, *Quarterly Journal of Economics* (1962); Hines, *Review of Economic Studies* (Oct 1964); H. A. Turner and D. A. Jackson, *Economic Journal* (Dec 1970); G. Pierson, *American Economic Review* (1968); A. Jones, *The New Inflation: The Politics of Prices and Incomes* and Burton, *Wage Inflation*, pp. 48–50.

27. Mulvey and Trevithick, *Scottish Journal of Political Economy* (Feb 1974).

28. Burton, *Wage Inflation*, p. 50.

29. Purdy and Zis, in *Inflation and Labour Markets*, ed. Laidler and Purdy, p. 58.

30. H. Turner, in *Do Trade Unions Cause Inflation?*, ed. Jackson, Turner and Wilkinson.

31. Mulvey and Trevithick, *Scottish Journal of Political Economy* (Feb 1974) pp. 225–7.

32. It is obvious, to take but one example, that the 'sociological' and 'Monetarist' explanations of the inflationary process are wholly incompatible. Nevertheless, each school of thought remains firmly convinced of the veracity of its opinions.

33. G. H. Phelps-Brown, *Three Banks Review* (Mar 1975) p. 19.

Chapter 10

1. A full résumé appears in the *Midland Bank Quarterly Review* (Aug 1973).

2. Opinion is divided as to whether there *was* a policy operating in 1956.

3. *The Attack on Inflation*, Cmnd. 6151 (London: H.M.S.O., 1975).

4. In fact none of these voluntary policies made any provision for powers of implementation.

5. For example between workers paid at time rates and workers paid at price rates, see pp. 115–16.

6. See, for example, A. Jones, *The New Inflation. The Politics of Prices and Incomes*; J. Pickering, *Economic Journal* (June 1971); or H. Clegg, *How to Run an Incomes Policy, and Why We Made Such a Mess of the Last One*.

7. National Board for Prices and Incomes, *Fifth General Report*.

8. See Clegg, *How to Run an Incomes Policy, and Why We Made Such a Mess of the Last One*.

9. Some commentators such as G. H. Phelps-Brown, *Lloyds Bank Review* (July 1973), see price controls as essential whereas others such as S. Weintraub, *Journal of Economic Issues* (Dec 1972), see them as largely unnecessary.

10. See Phelps-Brown, *Lloyds Bank Review* (July 1973) pp. 9–10.

11. For additional details see the *Midland Bank Review* (Aug 1973) pp. 16–17.
12. For further details see *The Economist* (13 Oct 1973).
13. See, for example, S. Weintraub, *Lloyds Bank Review* (Jan 1971); *The Economist* (Apr 1971); R. Allen, *National Westminster Bank Review* (Aug 1971); or B. Hollowood, *National Westminster Bank Review* (Aug 1970).
14. See Weintraub, *Journal of Economic Issues* (Dec 1972), and H. C. Wallich and S. Weintraub, *Journal of Economic Issues* (June 1971).
15. These problems are discussed more fully in M. Parkin, M. T. Sumner and R. A. Jones, 'A Survey of the Econometric Evidence of the Effects of Incomes Policy on the Rate of Inflation', in *Incomes Policy and Inflation*, ed. Parkin and Sumner.
16. Ibid. p. 5.
17. F. P. R. Brechling, 'Some Empirical Evidence on the Effectiveness of Prices and Incomes Policies', in *Incomes Policy and Inflation*, ed. Parkin and Sumner.
18. D. C. Smith, 'Incomes Policy', *Britain's Economic Prospects*, ed. R. E. Caves.
19. National Board for Prices and Incomes, *Third General Report*.
20. These and all ensuing results are expressed as actual changes in either weekly or hourly wage rates during policy-on periods (as defined by each individual investigator) as compared with predictions based upon policy-off periods.
21. R. G. Lipsey and J. M. Parkin, *Economica* (May 1970).
22. Parkin, *Economica* (Nov 1970).
23. K. F. Wallis, *Economica* (Aug 1971).
24. L. G. Godfrey, 'Some Comments on the Estimation of the Lipsey–Parkin Inflation Model', in *Incomes Policy and Inflation*, ed. Parkin and Sumner.
25. P. Burrows and T. Hitiris, *Bulletin of Economic Research* (May 1972).
26. M. T. Sumner, 'Aggregate Demand, Price Expectations and the Phillips Curve', in *Incomes Policy and Inflation*, ed. Parkin and Sumner.
27. Taylor, in *Incomes Policy and Inflation*, ed. Parkin and Sumner.
28. A. G. Hines, in *The Current Inflation*, ed. Johnson and Nobay.
29. Parkin, Sumner and Jones, in *Incomes Policy and Inflation*, ed. Parkin and Sumner, p. 13.
30. Ibid. p. 18.
31. F. Blackaby, *National Institute Economic Review* (Nov 1971). The same sentiments are expressed by L. Ulman and J. Flanagan, *Wage Restraint. A Study of Incomes Policy in Western Europe*, p. 223.

Chapter 11

1. A complete statistical breakdown is contained in D. Kern, *National Westminster Bank Review* (May 1974) p. 25.
2. Ibid. p. 26.

Chapter 12

1. The formal title of which is the Cambridge Economic Policy Group.
2. See, for example, *The Economist* (22 Mar 1975) pp. 30–1, and D. Kern, *National Westminster Bank Review* (Aug 1975).

3. See Curwen and Fowler, *Economic Policy*, ch. 6.
4. Ibid.

Chapter 13

1. See, for example, M. Friedman, *Monetary Correction.*
2. See, for example, J. Hughes, *Banker* (Oct 1974); P. J. Sheehan and D. S. Ironmonger, *Australian Economic Review* (4th qtr 1973); H. W. Arndt, *Australian Economic Review* (3rd qtr 1973); P. Robson, *National Westminster Bank Review* (May 1974); S. Page and S. Trollope, *National Institute Economic Review* (Nov 1974); R. Allen and D. Savage, *National Institute Economic Review* (Nov 1974); J. D. Whiteley, *National Institute Economic Review* (Nov 1974); J. H. Yang, *Federal Reserve Bank of St Louis Review* (Oct 1974), and A. Fishlow, *Brookings Papers on Economic Activity*, no. 1 (1974).
3. Page and Trollope, *National Institute Economic Review* (Nov 1974).
4. The best developed system being that of Brazil, see Fishlow, *Brookings Papers on Economic Activity*, no. 1 (1974).
5. Page and Trollope, *National Institute Economic Review* (Nov 1974) p. 46
6. Allen and Savage, *National Institute Economic Review* (Nov 1974) p. 71.
7. Friedman, *Monetary Correction*, pp. 29–30.
8. See Fishlow, *Brookings Papers on Economic Activity*, no. 1 (1974), and Yang, *Federal Reserve Bank of St Louis Review* (Oct 1974).

Bibliography

G. ACKLEY, 'The Contribution of Guidelines', in *Guidelines, Informal Controls and the Market Place*, ed. G. P. Schultz and R. Z. Aliber (Chicago University Press, 1966).

—, *Stemming World Inflation* (The Atlantic Institute, 1971).

—, 'An Incomes Policy for the 1970s', *Review of Economics and Statistics* (Aug 1972).

A. A. ALCHIAN, 'Information Costs, Pricing, and Resource Unemployment', in *Microeconomic Foundations of Employment and Inflation Theory*, ed. E. S. Phelps *et al.* (London: Macmillan, 1971).

— and B. KLEIN, 'On a Correct Measure of Inflation', *Journal of Money, Credit and Banking* (Feb 1973).

M. ALLAIS, 'A Restatement of the Quantity Theory of Money', *American Economic Review* (Dec 1966).

R. ALLEN, 'Concerning Incomes Policy', *Moorgate and Wall St Review* (Spring 1971).

—, 'A De-escalation Policy', *National Westminster Bank Review* (Aug 1971).

R. G. ALLEN, 'Changes in the Distribution of Higher Incomes', *Economica* (1958) pp. 14–25.

R. I. ALLEN and D. SAVAGE, 'Inflation and the Personal Income Tax', *National Institute Economic Review* (Nov 1974).

L. C. ANDERSEN, 'The State of the Monetarist Debate', *Federal Reserve Bank of St Louis Review* (Sep 1973).

— and K. C. CARLSON, 'A Monetarist Model for Economic Stabilization', *Federal Reserve Bank of St Louis Review* (Apr 1970).

A. ANDO and E. C. BROWN, 'Lags in Fiscal Policy', in *Stabilization Policies*, Commission on Money and Credit (Englewood Cliffs, N.J.: Prentice-Hall, 1963).

G. C. ARCHIBALD, 'The Phillips Curve and the Distribution of Unemployment', *American Economic Review*, papers and proceedings (May 1969).

—, 'The Structure of Excess Demand for Labour', in *Microeconomic Foundations of Employment and Inflation Theory*, ed. E. S. Phelps *et al.* (London: Macmillan, 1971).

—, R. KEMMIS and J. W. PERKINS, 'Excess Demand for Labour, Unemployment and the Phillips Curve: A Theoretical and Empirical Study', in *Inflation and Labour Markets*, ed. D. Laidler and G. Purdy (Manchester University Press, 1974) ch. 5.

V. ARGY, 'Rules, Discretion in Monetary Management, and Short-Term Stability', *Journal of Money Credit and Banking* (Feb 1971).

H. ARNDT, 'Competition, Price and Wage Flexibility, and Inflation, The German Experience', *Antitrust Bulletin* (Autumn 1972).

—, 'Inflation: New Policy Prescriptions', *Australian Economic Review* (3rd qtr 1973).

M. J. ARTIS, 'Monetary Policy in the United Kingdom: The Indicator Problem', *Bankers' Magazine* (Oct 1972 and Nov 1972).

— and F. BLACKABY, 'On Incomes Policy', *District Bank Review* (Mar 1968).

O. C. ASHENFELTER and G. E. JOHNSON, 'Bargaining Theory, Trade Unions, and Industrial Strike Activity', *American Economic Review* (Mar 1969).

—, G. E. JOHNSON and J. H. PENCAVEL, 'Trade Unions and the Rate of Change of Money Wages in United States Manufacturing Industry', *Review of Economic Studies* (Jan 1972).

R. AUERBACH and R. MOSES, ' "The Phillips Curve and All That": A Comment', *Scottish Journal of Political Economy* (Nov 1974).

G. L. BACH and J. B. STEPHENSON, 'Inflation and the Redistribution of Wealth', *Review of Economics and Statistics* (Feb 1974).

A. D. BAIN, *The Control of the Money Supply* (Harmondsworth: Penguin, 1970).

T. BALOGH, *Labour and Inflation*, Fabian Tract No. 403 (1970).

BANK OF ENGLAND, 'Competition and Credit Control', *Bank of England Quarterly Bulletin* (June 1971).

—, 'Does the Money Supply Really Matter?', *Bank of England Quarterly Bulletin* (June 1973).

C. R. BARRETT and A. A. WALTERS, 'The Stability of Keynesian and Monetary Multipliers in the United Kingdom', *Review of Economics and Statistics* (Nov 1966).

N. S. BARRETT, G. GERADI and T. P. HART, 'A Factor Analysis of Quarterly Price and Wage Behaviour for U.S. Manufacturing', *Quarterly Journal of Economics* (Aug 1974).

J. R. BARTH and J. T. BENNETT, 'The Role of Money in the Canadian Economy: An Empirical Test', *Canadian Journal of Economics* (May 1974).

P. S. BARTH, 'Unemployment and Labour Force Participation', *Southern Economic Journal* (Jan 1968).

R. BEAN and D. A. PEEL, 'A Quantitative Analysis of Wage Studies in Four U.K. Industries, 1962–1970', *Journal of Economic Studies* (Nov 1974).

D. M. BECHTER, 'Money and Inflation', *Federal Reserve Bank of Kansas City Review* (July–Aug 1973).

G. BELL, 'Incomes Policy. The British Experience', *Business Economics* (Jan 1971).

J. A. BISHPAM, 'The Current Inflation and Short-Term Forecasting', in *Incomes Policy and Inflation*, ed. M. Parkin and M. T. Sumner (Manchester University Press, 1972) ch. 13.

F. BLACKABY, 'Incomes Policy and Inflation', *National Institute Economic Review* (Nov 1971).

— (ed.), *An Incomes Policy for Britain* (London: Heinemann, 1972).

R. G. BODKIN, 'Wage and Price Formation in Econometric Models', in *Inflation and the Canadian Experience*, ed. N. Swan and D. Wilton (1971).

B. BOSWORTH, 'Phase II: The U.S. Experiment With An Incomes Policy', *Brookings Papers on Economic Activity*, no. 2 (1972).

—, 'The Inflation Problem During Phase III', *American Economic Review*, papers and proceedings (May 1974).

J. K. BOWERS, P. C. CHESHIRE and A. E. WEBB, 'The Change in the Relationship Between Unemployment and Earnings Increases: A Review of Some Possible Explanations', *National Institute Economic Review* (Nov 1970).

A. R. BRAUN, 'Wages in the United Kingdom: Has There Been a Shift in the Phillips Curve?', *International Monetary Fund Staff Papers* (Mar 1971).

—, 'Compulsory Arbitration as a form of Incomes Policy. The

Australian Case', *International Monetary Fund Staff Papers* (Mar 1974).

F. P. R. BRECHLING, 'The Relationship Between Output and Employment in British Manufacturing Industries', *Review of Economic Studies* (July 1965).

—, 'Some Empirical Evidence on the Effectiveness of Prices and Incomes Policies', in *Incomes Policy and Inflation*, ed. M. Parkin and M. T. Sumner (Manchester University Press, 1972) ch. 2.

—, 'Wage Inflation and the Structure of Regional Unemployment', in *Inflation and Labour Markets*, ed. D. Laidler and G. Purdy (Manchester University Press, 1974) ch. 7.

E. BREHMER and M. BRADFORD, 'Incomes and Labour Market Policies in Sweden 1945–70', *International Monetary Fund Staff Papers* (Mar 1974).

J. A. BRITTAIN, 'Some Neglected Features of Britain's Income Levelling', *American Economic Review*, papers and proceedings (May 1960).

M. BRONFENBRENNER, 'Statistical Tests of Rival Monetary Rules', *Journal of Political Economy* (Feb 1961).

— and F. HOLZMAN, 'Survey of Inflation Theory', *American Economic Review* (Sep 1963).

J. BROTHWELL, 'An Alternative Theoretical Explanation of the Phillips Curve Relationship', *Bulletin of Economic Research* (Nov 1972).

C. J. BRUCE, 'The Wage–Tax Spiral: Canada 1953–1970', *Economic Journal* (June 1964).

K. BRUNNER *et al.*, 'Fiscal and Monetary Policies in Moderate Inflation', *Journal of Money, Credit and Banking* (Feb 1973).

E. C. BUDD, 'Post-War Changes in the Size Distribution of Income in the U.S.A.', *American Economic Review*, papers and proceedings (May 1970).

— and D. F. SEIDERS, 'The Impact of Inflation on the Distribution of Income and Wealth', *American Economic Review*, papers and proceedings (May 1971).

A. E. BURGER, 'The Effects of Inflation', *Federal Reserve Bank of St Louis Review* (Nov 1969).

G. J. BURGESS and A. J. WEBB, 'The Profits of British Industry', *Lloyds Bank Review* (Apr 1974).

B. BURKITT, 'The Calculation of the Degree of Unionization', *British Journal of Industrial Relations* (Nov 1973).

A. F. BURNS, 'Money Supply in the Conduct of Monetary Policy', *Federal Reserve Bulletin* (Nov 1973).

—, 'Letter on Monetary Policy', *Federal Reserve Bank of St Louis Review* (Nov 1973).

P. BURROWS and T. HITIRIS, 'Estimating the Impact of Incomes Policy', *Bulletin of Economic Research* (May 1972).

J. BURTON, *Wage Inflation* (London: Macmillan, 1972).

T. F. CARGILL, 'An Empirical Investigation of the Wage-Lag Hypothesis', *American Economic Review* (Dec 1969).

J. A. CARLSON and M. PARKIN, 'Inflation Expectations', University of Manchester, mimeo. 73/05 (June 1973).

SIR F. CATHERWOOD, 'Some Observations on Inflation and Incomes Policy', in *The Current Inflation*, ed. H. G. Johnson and A. R. Nobay (London: Macmillan, 1971).

R. E. CAVES (ed.), *Britain's Economic Prospects* (Washington D.C.: The Brookings Institution, 1968).

M. CHATTERJI, 'Cost Inflation and the State of Economic Theory: A Comment', *Economic Journal* (Mar 1975).

C. CLARK, 'Inflation and Declining Profits', *Lloyds Bank Review* (Oct 1974).

H. CLEGG, *How to Run an Incomes Policy, and Why We Made Such a Mess of the Last One* (London: Heinemann, 1971).

T. CONGDON, 'Why Has Inflation Accelerated?', *National Westminster Bank Review* (Feb 1973).

—, 'The Counter-Inflation Programme: Can It Work?', *Bankers' Magazine* (Aug 1973).

J. CORINA, 'Incomes Policy. An International Survey', *Il Politico Rivista di Scienze Politiche* (Sep 1967).

B. A. CORRY and D. LAIDLER, 'The Phillips Relation. A Theoretical Explanation', *Economica* (May 1967).

— and J. A. ROBERTS, 'Activity Rates and Unemployment. The U.K. Experience: Some Further Results', *Applied Economics* (Mar 1974)

D. R. CROOME and H. G. JOHNSON (eds), *Money in Britain 1959–1969* (Oxford University Press, 1971).

A. CUKIERMAN, 'A Test of the "No Trade-off In the Long Run" Hypothesis', *Econometrica* (Nov 1974).

J. M. CULBERTSON, 'The Lag in Effect of Monetary Policy. A Reply', *Journal of Political Economy* (Oct 1961).

P. J. CURWEN and A. H. FOWLER, *Economic Policy* (London: Macmillan, 1975).

P. DAVIDSON and S. WEINTRAUB, 'Money As Cause and Effect', *Economic Journal* (Dec 1973).

M. DESAI, 'Growth Cycles and Inflation in a Model of the Class Struggle', *Journal of Economic Theory*, no. 6 (1973).

—, 'The Phillips Curve: A Revisionist Interpretation', *Economica* (Feb 1975).

J. J. DIAMOND (ed.), *Issues in Fiscal and Monetary Policy* (De-Paul University, 1971).

L. A. DICKS-MIREAUX, 'External Influences and Inflation in the United Kingdom', in *The Current Inflation*, ed. H. G. Johnson and A. R. Nobay (London: Macmillan, 1971) ch. 9.

— and J. C. R. DOW, 'The Determinants of Wage Inflation. United Kingdom 1946–1956', *Journal of the Royal Statistical Society* (1959).

N. DUCK, M. PARKIN, D. ROSE and G. ZIS, 'The Determination of the Rate of Change of Wages and Prices in the Fixed Exchange Rate World Economy, 1956–70', University of Manchester, mimeo. 74/04 (Mar 1974).

J. T. DUNLOP, 'Guideposts, Wages and Collective Bargaining', in *Guidelines, Informal Controls and the Market Place*, ed. G. P. Schultz and R. Z. Aliber (Chicago University Press, 1966).

J. EATWELL, J. LLEWELLYN and R. TARLING, 'Money Wage Inflation in Industrial Countries', *Review of Economic Studies* (Oct 1974).

O. ECKSTEIN, 'Money Wage Determination Revisited', *Review of Economic Studies* (Apr 1968).

— and T. A. WILSON, 'The Determinants of Money Wages in American Industry', *Quarterly Journal of Economics* (1962).

R. EISNER, 'What Went Wrong: Further Thought on Fiscal and Monetary Policy', in *Issues in Fiscal and Monetary Policy*, ed. J. J. Diamond (De-Paul University, 1971).

—, 'What Went Wrong?', *Journal of Political Economy* (June 1971).

G. J. EVANS, 'A Note on Trends in the Relationship Between Unemployment and Unfilled Vacancies', *Economic Journal* (Mar 1975).

D. FAND, 'Keynesian Monetary Theories, Stabilization Policy, and the Recent Inflation', *Journal of Money, Credit and Banking* (Aug 1969).

C. G. FANE, 'Index Linking and Inflation', *National Institute Economic Review* (Nov 1974).

W. H. FINK, 'Dollar Surplus and Devaluation', *Rivista Internazionale di Scienze Economiche e Commerciali* (July 1973).

I. FISHER, *The Purchasing Power of Money* (London: Macmillan, 1911).

A. FISHLOW, 'Indexing Brazilian Style: Inflation Without Tears?', *Brookings Papers in Economic Activity*, no. 1 (1974).

R. FLANAGAN and L. ULMAN, *Wage Restraint. A Study of Incomes Policies in Western Europe* (University of California Press, 1971).

M. FORES, 'Job Evaluation and Incomes Policy', *Lloyds Bank Review* (Oct 1974).

J. FOSTER, 'The Behaviour of Unemployment and Unfilled Vacancies. Great Britain 1958–1971: A Comment', *Economic Journal* (Mar 1973).

—, 'The Relationship Between Unemployment and Vacancies in Great Britain (1958–72): Some Further Evidence', in *Inflation and Labour Markets*, ed. D. Laidler and G. Purdy (Manchester University Press, 1974) ch. 6.

H. FOWLER, M. GILBERT and A. OKUN, *Inflation. The Problems it Creates and the Policies it Requires* (University of London Press, 1970).

D. R. FRANCIS, 'Proposed Solutions to Inflation – Effective and Ineffective', *Federal Reserve Bank of St Louis Review* (July 1971).

—, 'Has Monetarism Failed? – The Record Examined', *Federal Reserve Bank of St Louis Review* (Mar 1972).

—, 'Letter On Monetary Policy', *Federal Reserve Bank of St Louis Review* (Mar 1974).

—, 'How and Why Fiscal Actions Matter to a Monetarist', *Federal Reserve Bank of St Louis Review* (May 1974).

—, 'A Monetary Prescription for an Ailing Economy', *Federal Reserve Bank of St Louis Review* (June 1974).

—, 'The Role of Monetary Policy in Dealing With Inflation and High Interest Rates,' *Federal Reserve Bank of St Louis Review* (Aug 1974).

M. FRIEDMAN (ed.), *Studies in the Quantity Theory of Money* (Chicago University Press, 1956).

—, 'The Lag in Effect of Monetary Policy', *Journal of Political Economy* (Oct 1961), and 'Reply' (Oct 1969).

—, 'What Price Guideposts?', in *Guidelines, Informal Controls, and the Market Place*, ed. G. P. Schultz and R. Z. Aliber (Chicago University Press, 1966).

—, 'The Role of Monetary Policy', *American Economic Review* (Mar 1968).
—, 'Comment on Tobin', *Quarterly Journal of Economics* (May 1970).
—, 'Monetary Trends in the U.S.A. and in the U.K.', *American Economist* (Spring 1972).
—, *Monetary Correction* (London: Institute of Economic Affairs, 1974).
—, 'Letter on Monetary Policy', *Federal Reserve Bank of St Louis Review* (Mar 1974).
W. E. GIBSON, 'Price-Expectations Effects on Interest Rates', *Journal of Finance* (Mar 1970).
—, 'The Lag in Effect of Monetary Policy on Income and Interest Rates', *Quarterly Journal of Economics* (May 1970).
—, 'Interest Rates and Inflationary Expectations: New Evidence', *American Economic Review* (Dec 1972).
C. GILLION, 'Wage Rates, Earnings and Wage Drift', *National Institute Economic Review* (Nov 1968).
A. GLYN and B. SUTCLIFFE, *British Capitalism, Workers and the Profit Squeeze* (Harmondsworth: Penguin, 1972).
L. GODFREY, 'The Phillips Curve: Incomes Policy and Trade Union Effects', in *The Current Inflation*, ed. H. G. Johnson and A. R. Nobay (London: Macmillan, 1971) ch. 6.
— and J. TAYLOR, 'Earnings Changes in the United Kingdom 1954–70: Excess Labour Supply, Expected Inflation and Union Influence', *Oxford University Bulletin of Economics and Statistics* (Aug 1973).
H. N. GOLDSTEIN, 'Monetary Policy Under Fixed and Floating Exchange Rates', *National Westminster Bank Review* (Nov 1974).
J. F. GOODMAN, 'Strikes in the U.K.: Recent Statistics and Trends', *International Labour Review*, vol. 95 (1967).
R. J. GORDON, 'The Recent Acceleration of Inflation and its Lessons for the Future', *Brookings Papers on Economic Activity*, no. 1 (1970).
—, 'Steady Anticipated Inflation: Mirage or Oasis?', *Brookings Papers on Economic Activity*, no. 2 (1971).
—, 'Wage–Price Controls and the Shifting Phillips Curve', *Brookings Papers on Economic Activity*, no. 2 (1972).
—, 'The Response of Wages and Prices to the First Two Years of Controls', *Brookings Papers on Economic Activity*, no. 3 (1973).

H. GROSSMAN, 'Inflation. Union Aggressiveness or Inflationary Expectations?', *Bankers' Magazine* (June 1971).

—, 'The Cyclical Pattern of Unemployment and Wage Inflation', *Economica* (Nov 1974).

D. GUJARATI, 'The Behaviour of Unemployment and Unfilled Vacancies. Great Britain 1958–1971', *Economic Journal* (Mar 1972): also 'Reply', *Economic Journal* (Mar 1973).

—, 'A Reply to Mr Taylor', *Economic Journal* (Dec 1972).

G. HABERLER, 'Incomes Policy and Inflation. Some Further Reflections', *American Economic Review*, papers and proceedings (May 1972).

R. E. HALL, 'Prospects for Shifting the Phillips Curve Through Manpower Policy', *Brookings Papers on Economic Activity*, no. 3 (1971).

M. J. HAMBURGER, 'The Lag in the Effect of Monetary Policy: A Survey of Recent Evidence', *Federal Reserve Bank of New York Monthly Review* (Dec 1971).

D. S. HAMERMESH, 'Wage Bargains, Threshold Effects, and the Phillips Curve', *Quarterly Journal of Economics* (1970) pp. 501–17.

M. T. HAMILTON, 'Price Controls in 1973: Strategies and Problems', *American Economic Review*, papers and proceedings (May 1974).

B. HANSEN, 'Excess Demand, Unemployment, Vacancies and Wages', *Quarterly Journal of Economics* (1970).

R. A. HART, 'The Role of Overtime Working in the Recent Wage Inflation Process', *Bulletin of Economic Research* (1973) pp. 73–87.

J. HENNESSEY and F. PAISH, *Policy for Incomes*, Hobart Paper No. 29 (London: Institute of Economic Affairs, 1964).

J. R. HICKS, 'Real and Monetary Factors in Economic Fluctuations', *Scottish Journal of Political Economy* (Nov 1974).

—, *The Crisis in Keynesian Economics* (Oxford: Blackwell, 1974).

A. G. HINES, 'Trade Unions and Wage Inflation in the United Kingdom. 1893–1961', *Review of Economic Studies* (Oct 1964).

—, 'Wage Inflation in the United Kingdom 1948–1962. A Disaggregated Study', *Economic Journal* (Mar 1969).

—, 'The Determinants of the Rate of Change of Money Wage Rates and the Effectiveness of Incomes Policy', in *The Current Inflation*, ed. H. G. Johnson and A. R. Nobay (London: Macmillan, 1971) ch. 8.

—, 'Inflation and Economic Growth', in *Conflicts in Policy Objectives*, ed. N. Kaldor (Oxford: Blackwell, 1971) ch. 6.

—, 'The Micro-Economic Foundations of Employment and Inflation Theory: Bad Old Wine in Elegant New Bottles', *Discussion Paper No. 19*, Birkbeck College (Feb 1974).

— and C. NUSSEY, 'The International Monetarist Theory of Inflation. The Story of a Mare's Nest', *Discussion Paper No. 23*, Birkbeck College (Apr 1974).

R. HINSHAW (ed.), *Inflation As A Global Problem* (Baltimore: Johns Hopkins Press, 1972).

B. HOLLOWOOD, 'Price Control or Catastrophe', *National Westminster Bank Review* (Aug 1970).

—, 'It Could Happen Here', *National Westminster Bank Review* (May 1971).

J. M. HOLMES and D. J. SMYTH, 'The Relation Between Unemployment and Excess Demand for Labour: An Examination of the Theory of the Phillips Curve', *Economica* (Aug 1970).

C. C. HOLT, 'Improving the Labour Market Trade-Off Between Inflation and Unemployment', *American Economic Review*, papers and proceedings (May 1969).

—, 'Job Search, Phillips' Wage Relation and Union Influence: Theory and Evidence', in *Microeconomic Foundations of Employment and Inflation Theory*, ed. E. S. Phelps *et al.* (London: Macmillan, 1971).

—, 'How Can The Phillips Curve Be Moved to Reduce Both Inflation and Unemployment?', in *Microeconomic Foundations of Employment and Inflation Theory*.

H. HOUTHAKKER, 'Are Controls the Answer?', *Review of Economics and Statistics* (Aug 1972).

J. HUGHES, 'Are Threshold Agreements Inflationary?', *Banker* (Oct 1974).

D. JACKSON, H. TURNER and F. WILKINSON, *Do Trade Unions Cause Inflation?*, Department of Applied Economics, Occasional Paper No. 36 (Cambridge University Press, 1972).

H. G. JOHNSON, 'The Keynesian Revolution and the Monetarist Counter-Revolution', *American Economic Review*, papers and proceedings (May 1971).

—, 'Recent Developments in Monetary Theory: A Commentary', in *Money in Britain 1959-69*, ed. D. R. Croome and H. G. Johnson (Oxford University Press, 1971).

—, 'Notes on Incomes Policy and the Balance of Payments', in *Incomes Policy and Inflation*, ed. M. Parkin and M. T. Sumner (Manchester University Press, 1972) ch. 14.

—, *Inflation and the Monetarist Controversy* (Amsterdam: North-Holland, 1972).

— and P. Mieszkowski, 'The Effects of Unionization On the Distribution of Income: A General Equilibrium Approach', *Quarterly Journal of Economics* (Nov 1970).

— and A. Nobay (eds), *The Current Inflation* (London: Macmillan, 1971).

S. R. Johnson and P. E. Smith, 'The Phillips Curve, Expectations and Stability', *Quarterly Review of Economics and Business* (Autumn 1973).

J. Johnston, 'A Model of Wage Determination Under Bilateral Monopoly', in *Inflation and Labour Markets*, ed. D. Laidler and G. Purdy (Manchester University Press, 1974) ch. 3.

— and M. Timbrell, 'Empirical Tests of a Bargaining Theory of Wage Rate Determination', in *Inflation and Labour Markets*, ch. 4.

A. Jones, 'Prices and Incomes Policy', *Economic Journal* (Dec 1968).

—, *The New Inflation. The Politics of Prices and Incomes* (London: André Deutsch, 1973).

S. F. Kaliski, 'Is the Phillips Curve Still With Us?', in *Inflation and the Canadian Experience*, ed. N. Swan and D. Wilton (1971).

— and D. C. Smith, 'Inflation, Unemployment, and Incomes Policy', *Canadian Journal of Economics* (Nov 1973).

M. W. Keran, 'Monetary and Fiscal Influences on Economic Activity – the Historical Evidence', *Federal Reserve Bank of St Louis Review* (Nov 1969).

D. Kern, 'Monetary Policy and C.C.C.', *National Westminster Bank Review* (Nov 1972).

—, 'Public Sector Deficits', *National Westminster Bank Review* (May 1974).

—, 'Monetary Aspects of the Current Economic Debate', *National Westminster Bank Review* (Aug 1975).

J. M. Keynes, *A Treatise on Money* (London: Macmillan, 1930).

—, *The General Theory of Employment, Interest and Money* (London: Macmillan, 1936).

M. A. King, 'The United Kingdom Profits Crisis: Myth or Reality?' *Economica* (Feb 1975).

L. R. KLEIN, 'Empirical Evidence on Fiscal and Monetary Models', in *Issues in Fiscal and Monetary Policy*, ed. J. J. Diamond (De Paul University, 1971).

K. KNIGHT, 'Strikes and Wage Inflation in British Manufacturing Industry 1950–1968', *Bulletin of the Oxford University Institute of Economics and Statistics* (Aug 1972).

A. KNÖBL, 'Price Expectations and Actual Price Behaviour in Germany', *International Monetary Fund Staff Papers* (Mar 1974).

R. S. KOOT and D. A. WALKER, 'Rules Versus Discretion: An Analysis of Income Stability and the Money Supply', *Journal of Money, Credit and Banking* (May 1974).

R. K. KOSHAL and L. G. GALLAWAY, 'The Phillips Curve: An International Phenomenon', *Rivista Internazionale di Scienze Economiche e Commerciali* (July 1973).

M. KOSTERS, K. FEDOR and A. ECKSTEIN, 'Collective Bargaining Settlements and the Wage Structure', *Labour Law Journal* (Aug 1973).

E. KUH, 'A Productivity Theory of Wage Levels – An Alternative to the Phillips Curve', *Review of Economic Studies* (Oct 1967).

D. LAIDLER, 'The Phillips Curve, Expectations and Incomes Policy', in *The Current Inflation*, ed. H. G. Johnson and A. R. Nobay (London: Macmillan, 1971) ch. 5.

—, 'Monetarism, Stabilisation Policy and the Exchange Rate', *Bankers' Magazine* (Oct 1971).

—, 'The Current Inflation. Explanations and Policies', *National Westminster Bank Review* (Nov 1972).

—, 'Simultaneous Fluctuations in Prices and Output. A Business Cycle Approach', *Economica* (Feb 1973).

—, 'Monetarist Policy Prescriptions and Their Backgrounds', *Manchester School* (Mar 1973).

—, 'The Economy Mismanaged', *Banker* (Oct 1973).

—, 'The Influence of Money on Real Income and Inflation: A Simple Model With Some Empirical Tests for the United States 1953–72', *Manchester School* (Dec 1973).

—, 'Information, Money and the Macro Economics of Inflation', *Swedish Journal of Economics* (Mar 1974).

—, 'The 1974 Report of the President's Council of Economic Advisers: The Control of Inflation and the Future of the International Monetary System', *American Economic Review* (Sep 1974).

—, 'Economic Crisis 1974', *National Westminster Bank Review* (Nov 1974).

— and D. Purdy (eds), *Inflation and Labour Markets* (Manchester University Press, 1974).

R. F. Lanzillotti, and B. Roberts, 'The Legacy of Phase II Price Controls', *American Economic Review*, papers and proceedings (May 1974).

R. W. Latham and D. A. Peel, 'The Wage Variable and the Phillips Curve', *Scottish Journal of Political Economy* (Nov 1974).

F. de Leeuw and E. M. Gramlich, 'The Channels of Monetary Policy', *Federal Reserve Bulletin* (June 1969).

H. I. Liebling and A. T. Cluff, 'U.S. Postwar Inflation and Phillips Curves', *Kyklos*, vol. 22 (1969).

R. G. Lipsey, 'The Relation Between Unemployment and the Rate of Change of Money Rates in the United Kingdom 1862–1957', *Economica* (Feb 1960).

—, *An Introduction to Positive Economics*, 3rd edn (London: Weidenfeld & Nicolson, 1971).

— and M. Parkin, 'Incomes Policy. A Re-appraisal', *Economica* (May 1970).

— and M. Steur, 'The Relation Between Profits and Wage Rates', *Economica* (May 1961).

P. D. Lowe, 'An Inter-Industry Analysis of the Occlusion Between Profits and Threshold Wage Agreements in Provoking the Wage Price Spiral', University of Birmingham, Discussion Paper, Series A, no. 160 (Dec 1973).

R. E. Lucas, Jr and L. A. Rapping, 'Price Expectations and the Phillips Curve', *American Economic Review* (June 1969).

H. Lydall, 'The Long-term trend in the Size Distribution of Income', *Journal of the Royal Statistical Society*, Series A, vol. 122 (1959).

T. Lynes, *National Assistance and National Prosperity*, Occasional Papers on Social Administration, no. 5 (Codicote Press, 1962).

B. T. McCallum, 'The Effect of Demand on Prices in British Manufacturing. Another View', *Review of Economic Studies* (Jan 1970).

—, 'Rational Expectations and the Natural Rate Hypothesis: Some Evidence for the United Kingdom', *Manchester School* (Mar 1975).

T. W. McGuire and L. A. Rapping, 'Inter-industry Wage Change Dispersion and the "Spillover" Hypothesis', *American Economic Review* (June 1966).

—, 'The Determination of Money Wages in American Industry. Comment', *Quarterly Journal of Economics* (Nov 1967).

D. I. Mackay, 'After the "Shake-Out" ', *Oxford Economic Papers* (Mar 1972).

— and R. A. Hart, 'Wage Inflation and the Phillips Relationship', *Manchester School* (June 1974).

— and G. L. Reid, 'Redundancy, Unemployment and Manpower Policy', *Economic Journal* (Dec 1972).

B. G. Malkiel and E. J. Kane, 'Expectations and Interest Rates: A Cross-sectional Test of the Error-Learning Hypothesis', *Journal of Political Economy* (July–Aug 1969).

W. A. P. Manser, 'The Multinationals and Inflation', *Banker* (Nov 1974).

A. Marin, 'The Phillips Curve (Born 1958 – Died ?)', *Three Banks Review* (Dec 1972).

T. Mayer, 'The Lag in Effect of Monetary Policy. Some Criticisms', *Western Economic Journal* (Sep 1967).

J. Meade, *Wages and Prices in a Mixed Economy*, Occasional Paper no. 35 (London: Institute of Economic Affairs, 1971).

G. C. Means, 'Cost Inflation and the State of Economic Theory – Comment and Correction', *Economic Journal* (June 1974).

G. Meeks, 'Profit Illusion', *Oxford Bulletin of Economics and Statistics* (Nov 1974).

Midland Bank, 'The Use of Prices and Incomes Policies in Britain. The Search For a New Instrument', *Midland Bank Review* (Aug 1973).

—, 'Inflation and What To Do About It – A Survey of the Issues', *Midland Bank Review* (Nov 1974).

H. P. Miller, *Income Distribution in the U.S.*, 1960 Census Monograph (U.S. Government Printing Office, 1966).

D. Mitchell, 'A Simplified Approach to Incomes Policy', *Industrial and Labour Relations Review* (1969).

—, 'British Incomes Policy, the Competitive Effect and the 1967 Devaluation', *Southern Economic Journal* (July 1970).

— and A. R. Weber, 'Wages and the Pay Board', *American Economic Review*, papers and proceedings (May 1974).

F. Modigliani, 'Some Empirical Tests of Monetary Management, and of Rules Versus Discretion', *Journal of Political Economy* (June 1964).

D. T. MORTENSEN, 'A Theory of Wage and Employment Dynamics', in *Microeconomic Foundations of Employment and Inflation Theory*, ed. E. S. Phelps *et al.* (London: Macmillan, 1971).

J. MUELLBAUER, 'Prices and Inequality: The United Kingdom Experience', *Economic Journal* (Mar 1974).

C. MULVEY and J. A. TREVITHICK, 'Wage Inflation. Causes and Cures', *Central Bank of Ireland Quarterly Journal* (Winter 1970).

—, 'Trade Unions and Wage Inflation', *Economic and Social Review* (Jan 1973).

—, 'Some Evidence on the Wage Leadership Hypothesis', *Scottish Journal of Political Economy* (Feb 1974).

—, *The Economics of Inflation* (London: Martin Robertson, 1975).

N.B.P.I., *1st General Report*, Cmnd. 3807 (London: H.M.S.O., Aug 1966).

2nd General Report, Cmnd. 3394 (London: H.M.S.O., Aug 1967).

3rd General Report, Cmnd. 3715 (London: H.M.S.O., July 1968).

4th General Report, Cmnd. 4130 (London: H.M.S.O., July 1969).

5th General Report, Cmnd. 4649 (London: H.M.S.O., Apr 1971).

N.I E.S.R., 'Some Aspects of the Present Inflation', *National Institute Economic Review* (Feb 1971).

W. NORDHAUS, 'The Worldwide Wage Explosion', *Brookings Papers on Economic Activity*, no. 2 (1972).

A. NOVE, 'Cost Inflation and the State of Economic Theory – A Comment', *Economic Journal* (June 1974).

O.E.C.D., *Inflation. The Present Problems* (Paris, Dec 1970).

—, *Present Policies Against Inflation* (Paris, June 1971).

—, 'The International Transmission of Inflation', *Economic Outlook* (July 1973).

A. M. OKUN, 'Rules and Roles for Fiscal and Monetary Policy', in *Issues in Fiscal and Monetary Policy*, ed. J. J. Diamond (De Paul University, 1971).

—, 'The Mirage of Steady Inflation', *Brookings Papers on Economic Activity*, no. 2 (1971).

S. A. PAGE and S. TROLLOPE, 'An International Survey of Indexing and its Effects', *National Institute of Economic Review* (Nov 1974).

F. W. PAISH, *The Rise and Fall of Incomes Policy*, Hobart Paper No. 47 (London: Institute of Economic Affairs, 1967).

—, 'Business Cycles in Britain', *Lloyds Bank Review* (Oct 1970).

M. PALDAM, 'An Empirical Analysis of the Relationship Between Inflation and Economic Growth in 12 Countries, 1950–69', *Swedish Journal of Economics* (Dec 1973).

M. PANÍC and R. E. CLOSE, 'Profitability of British Manufacturing Industry', *Lloyds Bank Review* (July 1973).

M. PARKIN, 'Incomes Policy. Some Further Results on the Determination of the Rate of Change of Money Wages', *Economica* (Nov 1970).

—, 'The Phillips Curve: A Historical Perspective, Lessons From Recent Empirical Studies and Alternative Policy Choices', in *The Current Inflation*, ed. H. G. Johnson and A. R. Nobay (Macmillan, 1971) ch. 11.

—, 'The Short Run and Long Run Trade-offs Between Inflation and Unemployment in Australia', *Australian Economic Papers* (Dec 1973).

—, 'United Kingdom Inflation: The Policy Alternatives', *National Westminster Bank Review* (May 1974).

— and M. T. SUMNER (eds), *Incomes Policy and Inflation* (Manchester University Press, 1972).

—, M. T. SUMNER and R. A. JONES, 'A Survey of the Econometric Evidence of the Effects of Incomes Policy on the Rate of Inflation', in *Incomes Policy and Inflation*, ed. M. Parkin and M. T. Sumner (Manchester University Press, 1972) ch. 1.

—, M. T. SUMNER and R. WARD, 'The Effects of Excess Demand, Generalized Expectations and Wage–Price Controls on Wage Inflation in the U.K.', University of Manchester, mimeo. 74/02 (Jan 1974).

J. H. PENCEVAL, 'An Investigation into Industrial Strike Activity in Britain', *Economica* (Aug 1970).

—, 'A Note on the Comparative Predictive Performance of Wage Inflation Models of the British Economy', *Economic Journal* (Mar 1971).

—, 'Relative Wages and Trade Unions in the United Kingdom', *Economica* (May 1974).

G. L. PERRY, *Unemployment, Money Wage Rates and Inflation* (Massachusetts Institute of Technology Press, 1966).

—, 'The Success of the Anti-Inflation Policies in the United States', *Journal of Money, Credit and Banking* (Feb 1973).

M. PESTON, 'The Micro-Economics of the Phillips Curve', in *The*

Current Inflation, ed. H. G. Johnson and A. R. Nobay (London: Macmillan, 1971) ch. 7.

E. S. PHELPS, 'Phillips Curves, Expectations of Inflation and Optimal Unemployment Over Time', *Economica* (1967).

—, 'The New Microeconomics in Inflation and Employment Theory', *American Economic Review*, papers and proceedings (May 1969).

—, *et al.*, (ed.), *Microeconomic Foundations of Employment and Inflation Theory* (London: Macmillan, 1971).

—, 'Money Wage Dynamics and Labour Market Equilibrium', in *Microeconomic Foundations of Employment and Inflation Theory*, ed. E. S. Phelps *et al.* (London: Macmillan, 1971).

—, 'Inflation, Expectations and Economic Theory', in *Inflation and the Canadian Experience*, ed. N. Swan and D. Wilton (1971).

G. H. PHELPS-BROWN, 'Guidelines for Growth and for Incomes in the United Kingdom. Some Possible Lessons for the United States', in *Guidelines, Informal Controls and the Market Place*, ed. G. P. Schultz and R. Z. Aliber (Chicago University Press, 1966).

—, 'The Analysis of Wage Movements Under Full Employment', *Scottish Journal of Political Economy* (Nov 1971).

—, 'How Phase II worked in the U.S.A.', *Lloyds Bank Review* (July 1973).

—, 'New Wine in Old Bottles: Reflections on the Changed Working of Collective Bargaining in Great Britain', *British Journal of Industrial Relations* (Nov 1973).

—, 'A Non-Monetarist View of the Pay Explosion', *Three Banks Review* (Mar 1975).

A. W. PHILLIPS, 'The Relation Between Unemployment and the Rate of Change of Money Wage Rates in the United Kingdom 1861–1957', *Economica* (Nov 1958).

J. PICKERING, 'The Prices and Incomes Board and Private Sector Prices. A Survey', *Economic Journal* (June 1971).

G. PIERSON, 'The Effect of Union Strength on the U.S. Phillips Curve', *American Economic Review* (1968).

J. E. POWELL, 'Inflation and the Money Supply', *Banker* (Jan 1973).

A. R. PREST and D. J. COPPOCK (eds), *The U.K. Economy: A Manual of Applied Economics* (London: Weidenfeld & Nicolson, 1974).

D. L. PURDY and G. ZIS, 'Trade Unions and Wage Inflation in the U.K.', in *Inflation and Labour Markets*, ed. D. Laidler and G. Purdy (Manchester University Press, 1974) ch. 1.

—, 'On the Concept and Measurement of Union Militancy', in

Inflation and Labour Markets, ed. D. Laidler and G. Purdy (Manchester University Press, 1974) ch. 2.

RADCLIFFE, *Committee on the Working of the Monetary System*, Cmnd. 827 (London: H.M.S.O., 1959).

A. REES, 'The Phillips Curve as a Menu for Policy Choice', *Economica* (May 1970).

— and M. HAMILTON, 'The Wage–Price Productivity Perplex', *Journal of Political Economy* (1967) pp. 63–70.

G. L. REID, 'Redundancy, Unemployment and Manpower Policy', *Economic Journal* (Dec 1972).

D. ROBINSON, 'Implementing An Incomes Policy', *Industrial Relations* (Oct 1968).

P. ROBSON, 'Inflation-Proof Loans', *National Westminster Bank Review* (May 1974).

S. ROSEN, 'Trade Union Power, Threat Effects and the Extent of Organisation', *Review of Economic Studies* (1969) pp. 185–96.

M. ROSS, 'Guideline Policy. Where We Are and How We Got There', in *Guidelines, Informal Controls and the Market Place*, ed. G. P. Schultz and R. Z. Aliber (Chicago University Press, 1966).

K. W. ROTHSCHILD, 'The Phillips Curve and All That', *Scottish Journal of Political Economy* (Nov 1971).

—, 'Friedman, Expectations and the Phillips Trade-Off: A Reply', *Scottish Journal of Political Economy* (Nov 1974).

D. C. ROWAN, 'The Monetary System in the Fifties and Sixties', *Manchester School* (Mar 1973).

J. C. R. ROWLEY and D. A. WILTON, 'Quarterly Models of Wage Determination: Some New Efficient Estimates', *American Economic Review* (June 1973).

F. RUSHDY and P. J. LUND, 'The Effect of Demand on Prices in British Manufacturing Industry', *Review of Economic Studies* (Oct 1967).

P. SAMUELSON, 'Reflections on the Merits and Demerits of Monetarism', in *Issues in Fiscal and Monetary Policy*, ed. J. J. Diamond (De-Paul University, 1971).

J. D. SARGAN, 'A Study of Wages and Prices in the U.K. 1949–1968', in *The Current Inflation*, ed. H. G. Johnson and A. R. Nobay (London: Macmillan, 1971) ch. 4.

P. G. SAUNDERS, 'The Current Inflation: An Academic View', *Bankers' Magazine* (May 1973).

— and A. R. NOBAY, 'Price Expectations, the Phillips Curve and

Incomes Policy', in *Incomes Policy and Inflation*, ed. M. Parkin and M. T. Sumner (Manchester University Press, 1972).

J. SCHLESINGER, 'Monetary Policy and its Critics', *Journal of Political Economy* (Dec 1960).

G. P. SCHULTZ and R. Z. ALIBER (eds.), *Guidelines, Informal Controls and the Market Place* (Chicago University Press, 1966).

R. S. SCHULTZ, 'Clichés and Economics – The Myths of Inflation', *Business Economics* (May 1969).

C. L. SCHULTZE, 'Has the Phillips Curve Shifted? Some Additional Evidence', *Brookings Papers on Economic Activity*, no. 2 (1971).

M. SCOTT, 'A New Way to Attack Inflation', *Banker* (Apr 1974).

D. SEERS, *The Levelling of Incomes Since 1935* (Oxford: Blackwell, 1951).

A. K. SEVERN, 'Further Evidence on the Formation of Price Expectations', *Quarterly Review of Economics and Business* (Winter 1973).

S. S. SHALIT and M. BEN-ZION, 'The Expected Impact of the Wage–Price Freeze on Relative Shares', *American Economic Review* (Dec 1974).

P. J. SHEEHAN and D. S. IRONMONGER, 'The Real Income Guarantee: A Fiscal Policy to Control Inflation', *Australian Economic Review* (4th qtr 1973).

N. J. SIMLER and A. TELLA, 'Labour Reserves and the Phillips Curve', *Review of Economics and Statistics*, no. 1 (1968).

C. A. SIMS, 'Money, Income and Causality', *American Economic Review* (Sep 1972).

G. SIRKIN, 'Business Cycles Aren't What They Used to Be – And Never Were', *Lloyds Bank Review* (Apr 1972).

D. C. SMITH, 'Incomes Policy', in *Britain's Economic Prospects*, ed. R. E. Caves *et al.* (Washington D.C.: Brookings Institution, 1968).

—, 'Incomes Policy', in *Incomes Policy and Inflation*, ed. M. Parkin and M. T. Sumner (Manchester University Press, 1972).

W. L. SMITH, 'On Some Current Issues on Monetary Economics: An Interpretation', *Journal of Economic Literature* (Sep 1970).

R. M. SOLOW, 'The Case Against the Case Against the Guideposts', in *Guidelines, Informal Controls and the Market Place*, ed. G. P. Schultz and R. Z. Aliber (Chicago University Press, 1966).

—, *Price Expectations and the Behaviour of the Price Level* (Manchester University Press, 1969).

R. W. SPENCER and D. S. KARNOSKY, 'Curbing Price Expectations:

the Key to Inflation Control', *Federal Reserve Bank of St Louis Review* (May 1972).

J. L. STEIN, 'Unemployment, Inflation and Monetarism', *American Economic Review* (Dec 1974).

F. H. STEPHEN, 'Wage Determination and Trade Unions: A Comment', *Scottish Journal of Political Economy* (June 1974).

—, 'Wage Determination and Trade Unions: A Rejoinder', *Scottish Journal of Political Economy* (Nov 1974).

M. T. SUMNER, 'Aggregate Demand, Price Expectations and the Phillips Curve', in *Incomes Policy and Inflation*, ed. M. Parkin and M. T. Sumner (Manchester University Press, 1972) ch. 9.

—, 'The Current Inflation: A Programme For Control', *Bankers' Magazine* (May 1973).

M. J. C. SURREY, 'Money and the Multiplier', *Oxford Bulletin of Economics and Statistics* (Feb 1974).

N. SWAN and D. WILTON (eds), *Inflation and the Canadian Experience*, Industrial Relations Centre (Kingston, Ontario: Queen's University, 1971).

P. SYLOS-LABINI, 'Oligopoly, Unions and Inflation', in *Inflation and the Canadian Experience*, ed. N. Swan and D. Wilton (1971).

J. TAYLOR, 'Hidden Unemployment, Hoarded Labour, and the Phillips Curve', *Southern Economic Journal* (July 1970).

—, 'The Behaviour of Unemployment and Unfilled Vacancies. Great Britain 1958–1971. An Alternative View', *Economic Journal* (Dec 1972).

—, 'Incomes Policy, the Structure of Unemployment and the Phillips Curve: the United Kingdom Experience 1953–70', in *Incomes Policy and Inflation*, ed. M. Parkin and M. T. Sumner (Manchester University Press, 1972) ch. 10.

—, *Unemployment and Wage Inflation* (London: Longmans, 1974).

— and S. MCKENDRICK, 'How Should We Measure the Pressure of Demand?', *Lloyds Bank Review* (Jan 1975).

A. P. THIRLWALL, 'Demand Disequilibrium in the Labour Market and Wage Rate Inflation in the United Kingdom', *Yorkshire Bulletin* (May 1969).

—, 'Types of Unemployment in the Regions of Great Britain', *Manchester School* (Dec 1974).

R. L. THOMAS, 'Wage Inflation in the U.K. – a Multi-Market Approach', in *Inflation and Labour Markets*, ed. D. Laidler and G. Purdy (Manchester University Press, 1974).

—, 'The Cross-Sectional Phillips Curve', *Manchester School* (Sep 1974).

— and P. J. M. Stoney, 'Unemployment Dispersion As a Determinant of Wage Inflation in the United Kingdom, 1925–66', *Manchester School* (June 1971).

M. Thorning, 'Cyclical Fluctuations in Prices and Output in the United States, 1920–1970', *Economic Journal* (Mar 1975).

A. W. Throop, 'The Non-Union Wage Differential and Cost-Push Inflation', *American Economic Review* (Mar 1968).

D. G. Tipping, 'Price Changes and Income Distribution', *Applied Statistics*, vol. 19, no. 1 (1970) pp. 1–17.

J. Tobin, 'The Monetary Interpretation of History', *American Economic Review* (June 1965).

—, 'Money and Income: Post Hoc Ergo Propter Hoc?', *Quarterly Journal of Economics* (May 1970).

—, 'Inflation and Unemployment', *American Economic Review* (Mar 1972).

J. A. Trevithick, 'Keynes, Inflation, and Money Illusion', *Economic Journal* (Mar 1975).

D. Tucker, 'Bronfenbrenner On Monetary Rules. A Comment', *Journal of Political Economy* (Apr 1963).

H. A. Turner and D. A. Jackson, 'On the Determination of the General Wage Level – A World Analysis', *Economic Journal* (Dec 1970).

S. J. Turnovsky, 'Empirical Evidence on the Formation of Price Expectations', *Journal of the American Statistical Association* (Dec 1970).

— and M. L. Wachter, 'A Test of the "Expectations Hypothesis" Using Directly Observed Wage and Price Expectations', *Review of Economics and Statistics* (Feb 1972).

—, 'Real Wages, Employment and Inflation', in *Microeconomic Foundations of Employment and Inflation Theory*, ed. E. S. Phelps *et al.* (London: Macmillan, 1971).

R. Turvey, 'Some Features of Incomes Policy and Comments on the Current Inflation', in *The Current Inflation*, ed. H. G. Johnson and A. R. Nobay (London: Macmillan, 1971) ch. 12.

L. Ulman, 'Cost Push and Some Policy Alternatives', *American Economic Review*, papers and proceedings (May 1972).

—, 'Connective Bargaining and Competitive Bargaining', *Scottish Journal of Political Economy* (June 1974).

J. Vanderkamp, 'Wage Adjustment, Productivity and Price Change Expectations', *Review of Economic Studies* (Jan 1972).

H. C. Wallich and S. Weintraub, 'A Tax-Based Incomes Policy', *Journal of Economic Issues* (June 1971).

K. F. Wallis, 'Wages, Prices and Incomes Policies: Some Comments *Economica* (Aug 1971).

A. A. Walters, 'Quantitative Studies of Money, 1959–1969', *Bankers' Magazine* (Feb 1970).

—, *Money in Boom and Slump*, Hobart Paper No. 44 (London: Institute of Economic Affairs, 1970).

R. Ward and G. Zis, 'Trade Union Militancy as an Explanation of Inflation: An International Comparison', *Manchester School* (Mar 1974).

J. Waters, 'Money Supply and Credit in Theory and Practice', *National Westminster Bank Review* (Nov 1969).

S. Weintraub, 'A Feasible Anti-Inflation Incomes Policy', *Lloyds Bank Review* (Jan 1971).

—, 'Incomes Policy Completing the Stabilisation Triangle', *Journal of Economic Issues* (Dec 1972).

—, 'Cost Inflation and the State of Economic Theory – A Comment', *Economic Journal* (June 1974).

J. C. Weldon, 'Theoretical Penalties of Inflation', in *Inflation and the Canadian Experience*, ed. N. Swan and D. Wilton (1971).

J. P. Whitely, 'Mortgages; The Case for Index-Linking', *National Institute Economic Review* (Nov 1974).

M. Whitman, 'Economic Openness and International Financial Flows', *Journal of Money, Credit and Banking* (Nov 1969).

P. Wiles, 'Cost Inflation and the State of Economic Theory', *Economic Journal* (June 1973).

M. Willes, 'Lags in Monetary and Fiscal Policy', *Federal Reserve Bank of Philadelphia Review* (Mar 1968).

R. K. Wilkinson and B. Burkitt, 'Wage Determination and Trade Unions', *Scottish Journal of Political Economy* (June 1973).

—, 'Wage Determination and Trade Unions. A Reply', *Scottish Journal of Political Economy* (June 1974).

J. H. Williamson, 'The Price–Price Spiral', *Yorkshire Bulletin* (May 1967).

D. M. Winch, 'Inflation and Resource Allocation', in *Inflation and the Canadian Experience*, ed. N. Swan and D. Wilton (1971).

P. WOOD and J. RHYS, 'The Definition of Money and the Possibilities For Monetary Control', *Bankers' Magazine* (Apr 1971).

A. WOODFIELD, 'Job Search Costs and the Measurement of Structural Unemployment', *Scottish Journal of Political Economy* (Feb 1975).

J. H. YANG, 'The Case for and Against Indexation: An Attempt at Perspective', *Federal Reserve Bank of St Louis Review* (Oct 1974).

W. P. YOHE and D. S. KARNOSKY, 'Interest Rates and Price Level Changes 1952–69', *Federal Reserve Bank of St Louis Review* (Dec 1969).

Author Index

Subject Index